SAFE CHILD

~

DANGEROUS WORLD

A FAMILY SURVIVAL GUIDE

Ruth Lerner

Copyright © 2013 Ruth Lerner
All rights reserved.
Registration Number: TXu 1-861-119. Effective April 18, 2013.
Certification in name of Ruth Lerner.
ISBN: 1489533222
ISBN 13: 9781489533227

RUTH LERNER

SAFE CHILD

~

DANGEROUS WORLD

A FAMILY SURVIVAL GUIDE

DISCLAIMER

This handbook is intended as a helpful guide for families in their effort to keep their children safe. It is written with the understanding that the author is not engaged in providing professional services. The contents of each chapter reflect the information gathered by the author as well as the author's opinions about such information. Every effort has been made to make sure that the material in this handbook is correct. This handbook deals with a broad range of subjects related to child and family safety. It is not intended to replace the expert professional advice of psychologists, physicians, fire safety experts, emergency responders, police officers, water safety instructors or any other trained specialists. If the reader requires assistance or advice in a particular subject area, he or she should confer with a competent professional in the field.

The author is not responsible for the use or misuse of the information contained herein.

To Ilana
You are the inspiration for this book.
May you inspire others throughout your life.

ACKNOWLEDGEMENTS

I want to thank my sons, David Lerner and Matthew Ross, for their encouragement and help in writing this handbook. I'm not sure I would have had the stamina and motivation to get from start to finish without their collaboration. Matthew guided me through format issues, encouraged me to make the handbook more child friendly, and made suggestions that enhanced the content in many respects. David stressed that it's not enough to teach children a set of rules. Children should be taught to think on their feet when circumstances change and the rules may not apply. The chapters on bullying and child empowerment were based on David's experiences as a child and reflect the effort he is making to empower his five-year-old daughter, Ilana.

My daughter and son-in-law, Linda and Jay Zwicker, encouraged me and offered recommendations, which have been incorporated into this handbook. Jay, who is Board Certified in Security Management, has spent the better part of his professional career working in college campuses, educating students in security and safety matters. But their greatest contribution was in setting examples of excellent parenting. They are full-time working parents, but that didn't prevent them from raising my twenty-one-year old granddaughter, Mariah, to be a mature, smart, talented, independent, loving, generous, and absolutely delightful person.

Thanks to everyone who reviewed all, or portions of, the handbook. Janet Grossman of Sag Harbor, New York, had the patience to read, review, and edit the entire book, offering observations, corrections, and suggestions. She generally reserves her many-faceted talents to review her husband, Karl Grossman's, many writings, including his "Suffolk Close-up" column in *The East Hampton Press* and *The Southampton Press*, a column he's been writing for fifty years.

Thanks to Harriet Hellman, CPNP, PhD, AANP, director of Hampton Community Health Care in Water Mill, Long Island, New York, for taking some of her precious time to review the book.

Thanks to Russell Jonas, a volunteer fireman in the Hamptons since 1980, and Edward DiMonda, chairman of the board of the North Sea Fire Department, a fireman since 1957, who were kind enough to offer their input.

Thanks to Donald G. Kuss of the Bridgehampton Fire Department for his input.

Thanks to Paul Bollo, a real estate agent and resident of Southampton Village, New York, for suggesting a section on home pool safety. And finally, thanks to Molly Lambert, swimming instructor at the Southampton Youth Services pool for her cogent comments about water safety.

Contents

Preface: Why this handbook got written 1

Part I. Avoiding Danger in Public Places 9

Chapter 1 How to Stay Safe in a Public Space 11

Chapter 2 How to Stay Safe Crossing the Street 19

Chapter 3 How to Stay Safe
on or Near a School Bus 31

Chapter 4 How to Stay Safe in an Automobile 35

Chapter 5 How to Stay Safe at the Playground 47

Chapter 6 How to Stay Safe
Outdoors in the Summer 53

Chapter 7 How to Stay Safe in the Water 63

Part II. Dangers in the Home 79

Chapter 8. How to Avoid Accidents at Home 81

Chapter 9 Additional ways to Avoid
Injuries at Home 91

Chapter 10 How to Stay Safe In Case of Fire 95

Chapter 11 How to Prevent Carbon
Monoxide Poisoning 103

Chapter 12 How to Call for Help in an Emergency 109

Chapter 13 What to Do If Someone Is Choking 113

Part III Personal Dangers 123

Chapter 14 How to Be Safe on the Internet 125

Chapter 15 How to Prevent Bullying 127

Chapter 16 Empowering Your Child............................139

Appendix... 143

PREFACE

Young children have the amazing ability to absorb and retain large quantities of information and communicate that information to others. Three-year-olds can learn their names, addresses, telephone numbers, parents' names, and other crucial pieces of information. By four, children can recognize and handle dangerous situations inside the home and out.

I'm fortunate to share a home with a precocious five-year-old granddaughter who keeps me on my toes. We're best friends who share secrets and discuss virtually everything. As I taught her safety lessons, I realized that not every child has a mentor with time and energy to examine safety issues and explain them at a child's level of understanding.

Then I had an epiphany or, as I prefer to call it, my aha moment. "You've done the work. Why not share it with other families?" The question arose: How do I get this message to my target audience of preschool and elementary school-age children and their families?

My goal is to reach as many families as possible. I know that many households are comprised of two working parents or a single, self-supporting parent with little free time to spend on instruction beyond the obligatory help with homework assignments. In addition to these hardworking moms and dads, I'm counting on you—Grandma and Grandpa, Nana and Poppy, Abuela and Abuelo, Babcia and Dziadek,

Nonna and Nonno, etc. You, particularly if you're retired and live in relative proximity to your family, probably devote hundreds of hours each year to chatting, playing, and cuddling with your grandchildren. The time you're spending is, as it says in the ubiquitous commercial, *priceless*. If you invest a small portion of these precious hours imparting the life lessons spelled out in this handbook, your investment will be returned many times over. You will have helped raise a safe, self-confident, and empowered child. This is one grandparent's loving message, which I hope you'll help me share with this generation's young boys and girls. Keep in mind as you read this handbook that the advice offered for best practices may have to be adapted to meet differing situations which you and your family may encounter.

I retired from my position as manager of a large housing complex in Manhattan in 2002 and found I had free time on my hands. I joined a playwriting group, wrote a novel, and involved myself in other activities until 2008, when my granddaughter Ilana was born. With a grandmother's concern about the safety of her grandchildren and the time to do something about it, I made a conscious effort to bring myself up-to-date on child safety issues.

I have three terrific adult children and two wonderful granddaughters who were born sixteen years apart. When my children were born, I decked out their crib (the same one for all three) with bumpers, pillows, and a fluffy, down quilt. They slept on their stomachs. When my five-year-old granddaughter was born, my son David and his wife, Doris, did the exact opposite. The crib had no bumpers, no pillows, and, in the early months, only a light blanket wrapped snugly around her. She was put to sleep on her back.

Preface

Things change! Times change! Methods change! What was fashionable and thought to be correct in the sixties is considered unsafe today. Away with drop-down cribs and those baby contraptions with wheels and bumpers in which babies tooled around. There are warnings about leaving babies alone on changing tables and feeding them formula in toxic plastic bottles.

I read articles on child safety in newspapers and magazines. I watched news reports on TV and listened to twenty-four-hour radio news stations. I watched with horror the tragic daily occurrences, labeled as accidents, that took the lives of young children and their families. I realized that a good many of the purported accidents could be attributed to a lack of awareness, carelessness, or a total disregard for safety. I checked out hundreds of websites, read blogs, and observed events unfolding in my own community to try to determine how to keep a young child safe. And when my granddaughter was old enough, about three-and-one-half years of age, I had conversations with her about how to stay safe. Our daily dialogues are incorporated into *Safe Child~Dangerous World*.

As I wrote, I realized that a child is only as safe as a parent is aware and prepared. I expanded the scope of the handbook to address broader issues that impact on child safety. For example, if a parent doesn't know how to control a car in hazardous weather conditions or drives drunk or under the influence of drugs, the child will be endangered despite all the cautions about using seat belts and proper behavior in a vehicle. Or if the parents fail to install and/or maintain smoke or carbon monoxide detectors in the home, the child's chance of surviving a fire or gas leak diminishes greatly.

I added sections on the danger of carbon monoxide poisoning, how to handle driving emergencies, and even added a section on safely filling up a gas can. As I wrote, new dangers came to my attention, things I'd never even considered. They were added. By the time I was done, the handbook was twice its original size.

This handbook is designed to provide a young child with sufficient guidance to handle most potentially dangerous situations, with the emphasis on avoidance. It's divided into three sections. Part I examines hazards that lurk outside the home. Part II covers perils in the home. Part III is more personal in nature and more complex. It deals with issues that challenge today's youth: Internet safety, bullying and child empowerment.

Raising a child is a grave responsibility. Parents and caregivers owe it to their children to provide a safe, secure, and nurturing environment, as well as to train them in the art of self-protection. While we can teach young children to act responsibly, without parents and caregivers doing their parts, the efforts will be in vain. Safety and preparedness go hand in hand.

The handbook, in addition, offers simplified explanations of the causes of certain dangerous phenomena. For example, it explains how ocean rip currents are created and how static electricity causes explosions.

While the handbook provides basic instructions for calling 911 in an emergency, choking prevention techniques, and CPR, I strongly recommend the whole family take a professional safety course in these life-saving techniques. Our extended family recently completed such a course. During a three-hour class, my five-year-old granddaughter successfully learned to perform chest compressions, rescue breaths, and assemble and use an automated defibrillator.

Children's safety books tend to focus on avoidance of a specific risk: fire, drowning, stranger danger, bullying, etc. To get the whole picture, you'd have to amass a small library. I've incorporated these diverse subject areas into one comprehensive handbook. While it's virtually impossible to cover every potentially dangerous situation, I've dealt with those that children will generally encounter during their daily routines.

This handbook is not meant to be read in one or two sittings. It should be treated like an instruction manual or reference guide: kept in a handy spot to be read and reread. You may choose to read or reread a particular chapter depending on what occurred that day or what issue your child raises.

In most instances, the chapters are divided into two parts. The sections "In the Reading Room" are designed for children to read on their own (or for parents, grandparents, or other caregivers to read out loud). Read and discuss the content of these sections and then test the child's understanding with the questions in the Appendix and any other questions you or the child may raise. My granddaughter knows I am writing this book, and each day she tests *me* by asking me safety questions. For her, it's a game. For me, it's a confirmation of our family's view that it's never too early to teach a child important life lessons.

The portions of the handbook entitled "Important Information for the Parent, Grandparent, or Other Caregiver" cover the preventive and defensive steps parents need to take to keep their families safe. The reader should discuss pertinent information in this section with the child. The goal is to teach the child about coping with the dangers of daily living without instilling fear. For the child, knowledge is power.

Reinforce the handbook discussions by making your child's daily activities learning experiences. Point out safety issues as you and your child cross the street, ride in a car, play in a playground, shop at a mall, or enjoy a day at the beach. Walk through the rooms of your home and point out potential hazards and correct those identified.

Read. Discuss. Absorb. Test your child's knowledge by asking and answering questions. Review and practice your family's home escape plan. Accidents happen, but the number and severity can be dramatically reduced by giving your child or grandchild, niece or nephew the skills and knowledge to survive. It's truly much better to be safe than sorry.

Ruth Lerner

REAL LIFE SITUATIONS

September 1994
Southampton, N.Y. Tennis star died of carbon monoxide poisoning while napping in pool-house bedroom. Pool heater improperly vented. *Read Chapter 11.*

November 2011
Ridge Farm, Illinois. 10 year old honor student, taunted by classmates, hanged herself from a knitted scarf on a clothing rod in her closet. *Read Chapter 15.*

December 2011
Stamford, Connecticut. Home fire kills five people. Hot ashes and embers improperly disposed of. *Read Chapter 8.*

July 2012
Newport, New Hampshire. Toddler dies after falling into swimming pool. Police report pool's safety fence and gates were unsecured right before child was found. *Read Chapter 7.*

April 2013
Orofino, Idaho. An extension cord used to plug in an electric grill shorted, causing fire killing two adults and three teens. The cord was inadequate to carry the electric load. The house had no smoke alarms. *Read Chapter 10.*

IS YOUR FAMILY PREPARED?

Part I

Avoiding Danger In Public Places

CHAPTER 1

How to Stay Safe in a Public Place

IN THE READING ROOM

Timmy and Tammy are brother and sister. Actually, they're twins. They're six years old and will be starting first grade in the fall. They live in a nice town bordered by the ocean on one side and bays on the other. There are lots of trees and farms.

During the week, their grandma takes care of them while their mommy and daddy go to work. Grandma sends them to school on the school bus each day and meets them at the bus stop after school. Sometimes she drives them into town after school to do errands or just to walk around and look in the shop windows. Other days she lets them play outside the house, but keeps a close eye on them because she wants them to be safe.

On weekends, Mommy and Daddy take the twins to lots of places. Some trips are to fun places like parks and playgrounds. Others combine fun with doing chores, like going to the shopping mall. Mommy and Daddy also keep a close eye on the twins when they're in public places.

IMPORTANT INFORMATION FOR THE PARENT, GRANDPARENT, OR OTHER CAREGIVER

Keeping children safe requires more than just "watching" them. It's crucial that you alert your children to potential dangers, teach them how to avoid them, and, if avoidance is not an option, how to handle them.

IN THE READING ROOM

Mommy, Daddy, and Grandma teach Timmy and Tammy lots of ways to stay safe. The most important lesson the twins learned is: *never talk to strangers.*

A stranger is a person your family doesn't know. Timmy and Tammy will tell you that if you're approached by a stranger, an *imaginary alarm bell* should go off in your head, and you should run away from the stranger as fast as you can. This is not the time to worry about good manners! A stranger with *good* intentions would *not* approach you without the permission of the adult who is with you.

Timmy and Tammy know there's *never* a good reason for strangers to *invade their space* (get within touching distance of them). Mommy tells them to think of imaginary Hula-Hoops surrounding each of them. She warns, "Never let a stranger get close enough to get inside the make-believe hoop."

Daddy tells Timmy to imagine a *force field* surrounding him that will act as a shield to ward off danger. Daddy cautions Timmy to be *suspicious of strangers trying to enter his force field.*

Both twins are big fans of *Star Wars*. You'll often hear them say, "May the force be with you." Tammy asks Daddy if she can imagine a force field instead of a Hula-Hoop and he says that would be fine.

Daddy explains that the force field he is talking about is an *imaginary shield that surrounds each of them and protects them from attack.* Tammy asks how the force field can protect her, and Daddy explains that, just like animals, humans have *instincts* or *feelings* that warn them of approaching danger. These instincts are an internal warning system—one that is inside our heads. He tells the twins that, like animals, humans can sense when someone or something is a threat to their safety. Daddy calls these feelings *red flags,* which pop up in your head when something doesn't feel right. He says that if a stranger tries to start a conversation with you, your internal early warning system should go *Alert! Alert! Red flag*! Don't answer. Just get away as fast as you can.

Tammy asks her daddy for other examples of red flags. He says, "One major *red flag* would be a grown-up doing something to you that makes you feel uncomfortable and then telling you, 'Don't tell anyone.' Another would be if you see a grown-up in the playground who doesn't appear to be with a child. Your built-in warning system should kick in. *Stay away! Stay away!* If that same grown-up comes up to you and asks if you want to go with him or her to play with his or her daughter, the warning system in your head should scream out, *'Danger! Danger!'*" Daddy asks Tammy, "If that happens, what should you do?"

"Run to my mommy or daddy or someone else who can help me," she quickly replies.

Since there's no way to tell the difference between nice strangers and bad ones by looking at them, the best advice is to keep away from *all* strangers. Daddy reminds the twins, "It's your mission to do everything you can to keep a stranger outside your force field." Daddy explains that *bad* strangers want to take you away from your family and might try to trick you into going with them. "Sometimes one may offer to tell you a secret or promise to give you money, candy, ice cream, or other treat. Or offer to let you see a puppy or ask for your help with a hurt animal or offer you a ride home."

Timmy shouts, *"We know these tricks and we won't fall for them! Even if the stranger knows our names, we won't go."*

Tammy chimes in, *"Even if the stranger tells us, 'Your mommy sent me,' we won't go!"*

Then Grandma gets into the act like a momma bear hovering over her baby cubs. "Remember," she says, "If a stranger tries to enter your force field and attempts to touch you, do whatever you have to do to get away. Scream, 'Stranger!' If the stranger is holding you, hit, kick, claw, and squirm out of your jacket. Do whatever it takes to call attention to yourself and run, run, run to Mommy, Daddy, or me. If you can't find us, run to where there are lots of people and ask a *trustworthy* adult for help. A trustworthy adult is someone who is in a position of authority, like a police officer, or who is a responsible person with the ability to help."

Tammy asks, "Grandma, how do I find a trustworthy adult?"

Grandma tells her that in a store, mall, or parking lot, a trustworthy adult can be an employee, a security guard, a police officer, or a parent with children. On the street, it may be a police officer, storekeeper, restaurant, or office employee. In a playground or park, look for parents with children.

Mommy tells Timmy and Tammy not to go alone to a public restroom. She tells them not to walk near cars in a parking lot, and if they think a car is following them, to turn and walk or run in the opposite direction. She reminds them not to wander off or play hiding games where they can't be seen.

Tammy says, *"Yeah, that's how you get in big trouble. Remember, Timmy, if you can't see Mommy, Mommy can't see you."* Tammy also says it's important that you and your parents share a *secret code*. If a stranger approaches you and doesn't know the *code*, you'll know your parents didn't send him or her.

Timmy whispers, "And don't tell anyone the code."

Tammy nods her head and responds, "If I tell someone the code, it won't be a secret anymore."

There's one more valuable lesson Timmy and Tammy learned that they want to pass on to you. **This** *may be one of the most important things you'll ever learn. Whether you're in a mall, store, doctor's office, playground, private home, school, camp, or any other place, the twins want you to know that if any adult asks you to do something you think is wrong or that makes you feel uncomfortable, it's absolutely, positively OK to say, "No" and tell someone immediately. Even if the adult is a family member, babysitter, nanny, family friend, neighbor, teacher, bus driver, or other person close to your family, don't be embarrassed, ashamed, or afraid. Act at once. Don't wait! Be brave and smart and the force will be with you.*

Remember, if you feel threatened, *scream*! Tell a trustworthy adult right away, and, if you have a cell phone, call 911 for help. In a later chapter, you'll learn how to call 911 and what to say when the operator answers.

CHAPTER 2

How to Stay Safe Crossing the Street

IMPORTANT INFORMATION FOR THE PARENT, GRANDPARENT, OR OTHER CAREGIVER

An accident, theoretically, is something that happens *unexpectedly* and *unintentionally.* Yet many collisions we call *accidents* aren't accidental at all. They could have been avoided if drivers, bike riders, and pedestrians exercised greater caution and better judgment.

People drive dangerously. It's a fact. Just stand on a street corner and watch drivers as they pass. You'll see them chatting on their cell phones, texting, using navigation systems (GPS), putting on makeup, reading papers, leaning over to adjust the radio, drinking scalding hot coffee, eating donuts, talking or arguing with passengers, and even shaving with electric razors. These drivers are doing everything *except keeping their minds and eyes on the road*. Many of them are just daydreaming, significantly slowing their reaction times.

When you come upon an *accident*, you'll generally hear the driver say, "I didn't see the light change," or "The car in front of me stopped short." No one ever says, "I wasn't paying attention."

In a 2013 survey of over six hundred parents conducted by researchers from the University of Michigan, close to 90 percent said they had used at least one technology-based distraction in the prior month while their children were in the car.

Some drivers engage in even more dangerous behavior. Every day we read about people driving drunk or high on prescription or other drugs, which impairs their judgment as well as their reaction times. Others are in a hurry or are sleep-deprived, as in the case of long-distance truck and bus drivers who are exhausted from being on the road too long. Even parents who work long hours or have an infant keeping them awake at night, can be sleep-deprived. Sometimes vehicles are not maintained and cannot stop because the brakes failed.

It's scary out there for adults as well as for children. Wouldn't it be wonderful if we could wrap our children in magic bubbles when they leave the house so they are always protected from bumps, bruises, mishaps, incidents, and accidents? Outside the house is a danger zone. Think about the range of things your child must know just to navigate the streets. *It's not enough to teach a child a set of rules. For every rule, there's an exception, a time when the rule can't apply.* We can teach children to cross when the traffic signal is green, but how do we prepare them to cross when the electricity goes out and there's no working traffic signal—or, for that matter, at busy intersections with no light? What do we tell children to do when they hear an ambulance, fire truck, or police car siren as they're crossing? What should they do when a police officer waves them across the street, but the light is red? What about when a driver smiles and waves for the child to cross, unaware that another car (whose driver is oblivious to the child's presence) is advancing in the next lane? How should the child react when a driver signals to make a right turn, and suddenly decides to go straight through the intersection? What rules govern these situations?

We know we can't conjure up magic bubbles or force fields to protect our children. We can, however, teach them to obey the rules, and provide them with mental checklists to draw upon when the rules don't apply.

IN THE READING ROOM

Timmy and Tammy love to spend time in town with their grandma, particularly when she takes them to the toy store and the ice cream parlor. They know

that she holds their hands while crossing the street to keep them safe. They listen carefully when Grandma teaches them how to use crosswalks, signal lights, and stop signs.

Timmy asks his grandma, "What's a crosswalk?"

Grandma tells him, "A crosswalk is a path for pedestrians (walkers), to use when crossing the street. Drivers expect to find people crossing at crosswalks, so they know to stop for them. A crosswalk has white lines on each side and white stripes painted from side to side. It looks like a ladder painted on the ground. Crosswalks are usually at a corner, but may be in the middle of a long block with a sign telling drivers to stop to let people cross."

Grandma says, "*Never* cross in the middle of a block unless there's a crosswalk and *never* cross between parked cars."

How to Stay Safe Crossing the Street

Tammy watches the signal lights change as they wait at the corner of a busy intersection. She asks Grandma, "How do I know when to cross?"

Grandma tells the twins that signal lights change from green to yellow to red and back to green. Green means *Go,* red means *Stop,* and yellow means *Caution.* The yellow caution light warns you that the light is about to turn red.

Sometimes you'll see a *Walk/Don't Walk* signal instead. When the word *Walk* lights up, you can cross. When the words *Don't Walk* light up, stay on the sidewalk. Never cross when the light is blinking. A blinking light tells you it is about to change. Instead of the words *Walk* and *Don't Walk* you might see a signal light with the image of a person walking, which means you can cross. An open red hand means you should wait.

Timmy asks what he should do if he's almost across the street when the signal starts to blink. Grandma tells him there should be enough time to finish crossing , but he should be very careful.

Tammy tells Timmy that if he hasn't started crossing yet, or if he is just stepping off the curb when the light starts to blink, he better get back on the sidewalk and wait for the signal to change back to green or for the word *Walk* or the image of the walking person to light up. Grandma applauds and tells Tammy she is a smart child.

Grandma and the twins cross the street and walk to the next block, which has a stop sign on each of the four corners. The twins aren't sure what they should do. Grandma says that before you start to cross a street with a stop sign (or a street or road where there is no signal light, crosswalk, or stop sign), try to make eye contact with the drivers to make sure they see you and bring their cars to a full stop. When you step off the curb, look left, right, and left again. Look out for all cars, including those that may be turning into the street. Look both ways even on a one-way street. Grandma says, "That's a lot to think about, but with practice, you'll be fine."

Grandma gives Timmy and Tammy some more good advice:

- Always obey a crossing guard.
- Never use a cell phone or other electronic device when you're crossing the street.
- Never wear earphones when you're crossing the street. It's important to hear street sounds such as honking horns; motors racing; or ambulance,

police car, or fire truck sirens. Hearing these sounds can help you avoid potential danger. Sometimes you can hear a car coming before you see it.
- Don't wear hoods or ski masks that block your vision.
- Be extra cautious in bad weather. Streets may be icy and cars might have difficulty stopping.

Timmy tells Tammy it's important to learn about road signs. He saw a picture book in the school library that showed different types of signs. He learned that road signs let you know what's coming up ahead and that signs have different shapes and colors for different purposes. For example, a diamond-shaped sign is a warning. You'll find signs at railroad crossings, underpasses, dead ends, construction zones, and at many other locations.

"That was the easy part," Grandma tells the twins when they finish learning the safety rules.

She wishes she could conjure up a magic bubble or force field to protect the twins from situations when they're obeying the rules but *drivers are not.* Or when the electricity goes out and the traffic signals don't work. Or when the sign says *pedestrian crossing,* but the drivers don't stop. Or when the light is red, but the police officer or crossing guard waves them across the street.

Timmy asks Grandma, "How do I know when I have the right of way to cross the street?" The twins and their family live in New York State. Grandma tells the twins that the New York Safety Council says that *no one has the right of way*. The right of way must be yielded, depending on the circumstances. Most states have similar laws, she says. Grandma tells them that the law provides that drivers must yield to pedestrians using crosswalks, and if a pedestrian steps into the crosswalk, even if the light turns green for the driver, he must wait for the pedestrian to cross. Drivers making a turn, must also yield to pedestrians in crosswalks.

Grandma tells them that police officers, crossing guards, and emergency personnel have the authority to direct traffic. If they wave you across the street or tell you to wait, you must obey them, regardless of traffic signals or signs.

Grandma knows there will be countless other unexpected, potentially dangerous street situations that the twins will face as they grow up. She'll have to settle for teaching them to use their senses and their best judgment to stay out of harm's way. She'll provide them with a mental checklist to call up when the usual rules don't apply. Their safety will depend on their ability to consider their options and choose the best one.

Safety Checklist

STOP, LOOK, LISTEN, WAIT, GO

STOP: when you get to a corner.
LOOK: to see if any cars, trucks, buses, or other vehicles are coming.
LISTEN: for sirens, horns honking, motors racing, or tires screeching.
WAIT: until vehicles are stopped or there are no vehicles in your path.
GO: but stay alert. Always think one step ahead.

Timmy and Tammy look at each other and then tell Grandma, "Crossing the street is much harder than we thought. We think we'll just hold your hand until we turn ten."

Grandma laughs and hugs them both. She holds their hands as they walk to the park. While they're eating the lunch Grandma packed for them, she thinks it's a good time to discuss bicycle safety. It won't be long before the twins will be old enough to ride their bikes in town. She wants to make sure they know the rules. These are the pointers she gives them as they gobble down their sandwiches and slurp their milk through squiggly straws.

"If I had my wish," she says, "You'd never ride your bicycles on the road. I'd like to see your daddy take your bikes to the park or any other location where you can ride free of traffic and out of harm's way. But I don't expect that I can hold you back forever, so let's talk about bicycle safety."

Bicycle Safety

- Don't ride in the street without adult supervision unless your parents feel you are old enough to do so.
- Have a mirror, light, and reflectors on your bicycle.
- Wear a helmet and bright-colored or reflective clothing.
- If there's a bike lane, use it. Ride single file when riding with others.

How to Stay Safe Crossing the Street

- At busy intersections, walk your bicycle across the street.
- Obey all signal lights and stop signs.
- Ride in the direction of traffic.
- Stay in your lane. Never ride between lanes.
- Use hand signals for turns, lane changes, and stops.
- Don't ride close to parked cars. Doors can swing open and hit you.
- Keep both feet on the pedals and both hands on the handlebars.

Finished with their lunch and grandma's review of bicycle safety rules, Timmy and Tammy head over to the recently built scooter park. They each have a new razor scooter which their parents bought them for their birthday. The twins know that they have to wear protective gear when they use the scooters. Their parents gave them special helmets and elbow and knee pads for their birthday as well. Their scooters come equipped with a hand brake. The ones that don't require the child to drag his foot on the back tire in order to stop. Mom and Dad told the twins that could only ride their scooters at the scooter park. Dad warned them to be very careful to keep fingers and toes away from the folding hinge.

"Happy scooting, kids" Grandma called out. I'll be right here on the bench watching you.

CHAPTER 3

How to Stay Safe on or Near a School Bus

IN THE READING ROOM

Each weekday morning Grandma walks Timmy and Tammy to the school bus. The bus stop is about a block from their house and there is no sidewalk, so they have to walk on the shoulder of the road. Grandma worries about the twins taking the bus to and from school, and teaches them how to be as safe as possible.

Grandma tells them that they are more at risk going to or *near* a school bus than they are on it. She says they're too young to walk to the bus stop by themselves so she walks them to the bus stop in the morning, waits for them to get settled on the bus, and meets them at the bus stop after school. Grandma makes the twins get ready early so they won't have to rush. She says rushing results in accidents.

Timmy and Tammy can tell you how to be safe going to and coming home from school, just the way Grandma told them:

- Walk on the sidewalk, or, if there is no sidewalk, walk on the shoulder of the road *facing* traffic.
- If you're wearing a scarf or drawstring sweatshirt, or if you are carrying anything with straps that can get caught on the bus handrails or doors, tuck them in before getting on or off the bus.
- Stand back from the curb as the school bus pulls up.
- Never bend down near or under the bus wheels to try to pick something up. *This rule also applies to trucks, regular buses, and other vehicles.*
- When the driver opens the bus door and says it's OK, hold the handrail while you get on.
- When you get on the bus, find a seat, sit down, and face forward.

How to Stay Safe on or Near a School Bus

- Never stick your arms, legs, or head out of the bus window.
- Know the driver's name and your bus number.
- Respect the driver. Don't make loud noises or run in the aisle. Driving a school bus is tough enough without distractions.
- Keep the aisle clear of backpacks and other items to avoid creating a tripping hazard.
- Stay in your seat until the bus comes to a complete stop.
- Line up to get off the bus. Don't push or play around.
- Make sure you take your backpack and other items with you.
- Hold onto the handrail while you get off.
- When you get off the bus, look outside, toward the back of the bus, before you step down, just in case a car or bicycle is coming on the shoulder.
- Meet your parent or caregiver at the school bus stop.
- Never go back on the bus, even if you forget something.
- Never walk behind the bus.
- If you have to cross the street in front of a school bus, keep at least ten giant steps away from the

front so the driver can see you. Wait for the driver to wave you across, and, before you step out, look carefully to see if any cars are coming in either direction.

Evacuating a school bus in case of fire or accident. Timmy and Tammy's elementary school has a program of emergency drills on a school safety bus. They learn how to exit safely from the emergency rear door, emergency window exits, and the emergency roof hatch. If your school doesn't have a program to teach you how to escape from the bus in an emergency, your parents should ask the school board to set one up.

Remember: observe every bus rule to and from school.

CHAPTER 4

How to Stay Safe in an Automobile

IMPORTANT INFORMATION FOR THE PARENT, GRANDPARENT, OR OTHER CAREGIVER

Think about it. You can teach children passenger safety rules from now to eternity, but when they're in a car, they're at the mercy of the drivers. There are no magic circles or force fields that can insulate your child from driver error or dangerous driving habits. Your child's safety depends on the skill and knowledge of the driver of the car and, to a large extent, on the other drivers in the neighborhood who either drive carefully or tailgate, pass on shoulders, speed through intersections, send wrong turn signals, drive distractedly, etc. The following section offers guidance to children about what they can do to protect themselves. The rest is in your hands.

IN THE READING ROOM

Eddie lives in a private house in small city with his stay-at-home dad, who writes children's picture books about dinosaurs. His mom lives in an apartment complex on a busy street in a big city. His dad and mom are divorced, and his mom lives and works over two hours away. On weekends, Dad takes Eddie to visit Mom. They spend a lot of time in the car, and Dad is concerned about Eddie's safety. As soon as they get in the car, Dad makes sure Eddie is buckled up.

As Dad drives on the highways and busy streets to and from Mom's apartment, they talk about car safety rules. Some rules are general and can be applied to other situations, such as riding on a bus. Others are specifically about being a passenger in a car. What Eddie learns applies to all children.

Dad tells Eddie, *"Never get into a car with a stranger. You should apply the same stranger danger rules you would follow in public places. And, Eddie, I don't know how to emphasize this enough. Never get into a car with a drunk driver, even if the driver is your mom, dad, grandparent, caregiver, or other person. Not anyone!"*

How to Stay Safe in an Automobile

Dad tells Eddie, "You have to do your part to keep safe. In the car, sit in your car seat facing front. Buckle up. Behave yourself. Don't distract the driver. Remember, if I'm yelling at you, my attention is on *you*, *not* on the road."

Use Car Seats, Booster Seats, and Safety Belts.

As soon as you get into the car, get into your car seat and *strap in.* Lock the lap and shoulder belts. Your seatbelt will keep you from being thrown around in a sudden stop or crash. If you don't know how to use the seat belts, ask your parent or caregiver to teach you. You must know how to open the belt in an emergency. If your parents forget to strap you in, tell them to do so before starting the car.

Make sure the shoulder strap fits snugly across your chest and shoulder. In warm weather, when you're no longer wearing a jacket, make sure someone adjusts the straps to fit snugly.

Booster Seats.

If you've outgrown your car seat and are under twelve years of age, you should ride in the backseat using a booster seat, which raises you up so the car's seat belt fits securely across your chest. In lots of places, this is more than a rule. It's the law. Keep in mind that sometimes emergencies happen where a parent or other adult has to drive several children home from school or an outing. The car may have only one car or booster seat. In such a case, if there is no special seat for you, sit in the backseat and buckle the safety belt, pulling it snugly across your chest.

If you are under thirteen years, avoid riding in the front seat of a car if at all possible. According to the Center for Disease Control & Prevention (CDC), air bags can kill young children riding in the front seat. If the circumstances are such that you *must* sit in the *front* seat in an emergency situation, ask the driver to push your seat all the way back from the dashboard and buckle the safety belt. Don't lean forward. Stay as far back from the dashboard as you can. *Remember, if at all possible, don't sit in the front seat.*

Learn how to open the car windows, but never do so unless it's absolutely necessary.

How to Stay Safe in an Automobile

Never put your head, arms, or legs out of an open car window or sunroof.

When getting in and out of the car, keep your hands and feet clear of the doors, and before you close a car door, check that everyone else's hands and feet are clear of the door.

Eddie's dad offers other tips for keeping safe that can save your life:

- *Never* stay alone in a car with the windows closed, especially when the engine is running. *Never*! Not in the garage, parking lot, driveway, or on the street.
- Ask the driver *not* to leave you alone in the car while doing errands, particularly when the engine is running. There are two reasons for this rule:
  1. When a car engine is running, it gives off carbon monoxide fumes, which are very dangerous. If the car's tailpipe gets clogged (with sand or snow or other blockage), the fumes will come into the car.
  2. A car left with the engine running is a temptation for a car thief. Sometimes a bad person will try to steal the car while the driver is

inside a store or otherwise away from the car. It's much easier to steal a car with the key in it. The thief may not even realize you're in the backseat.
- Never stand behind or on the side of a car when the driver starts the engine. You are short and you may be in his *blind spot*. A blind spot is a section of the car where the driver can't see you in his mirrors. He won't know to stop as he backs out of the driveway or a parking spot.
- Be aware of traffic around you as you ride in the car. Be a helpful passenger. If you see something that could be dangerous and you think the driver doesn't see it, mention it. Don't shout. Say it calmly.
- Pay attention to sounds around you. For example, highways have *rumble strips* on the shoulder to alert a driver that the car is drifting off the road. Frequently, there are rumble strips in the centerline of the road to alert a driver when the car is drifting into the oncoming lane. When the tires touch the strip, it causes vibration and a loud rumbling noise designed to get the driver's attention. *If you hear the rumble, make sure the driver hasn't fallen asleep at the wheel.* Drowsy driving happens to every driver at one time or another.

IMPORTANT INFORMATION FOR THE PARENT, GRANDPARENT, OR OTHER CAREGIVER

How to stay safe if your car breaks down on the highway.

In the earlier section of this chapter, I said that a child's role in keeping safe in a car was limited and *the rest is up to you.* This portion of the chapter deals with the parents' roles in protecting the child (and the whole family) from danger that results from poor weather conditions, car trouble, and other hazardous situations.

Parents, have your car checked prior to taking long car trips. Long trip or short, make sure your car contains the items needed to handle an emergency. AAA offers suggestions for a winter survival kit including an ice scraper and brush, coffee can furnace, boots, gloves and hat, a tool kit (screwdriver, pliers, duct tape and adjustable wrench) a flashlight, tire traction material (sand or cat litter), non-perishable food, blankets, jumper cables, first aid kit, flares or reflective triangle and a shovel. Among other items they recommend are drinking water, a cell phone and charger, pencil and paper, candles and waterproof matches, a jack with a board for soft surfaces, lug wrench, umbrella and extra fuses.

If you have bouts of low blood sugar, keep a supply of suitable food to keep the level up. Test your blood glucose levels before starting to drive.

Keep something white in the car to use as a flag in the event the car breaks down. Over the last few years, in parts of the country that experienced either flooding or blizzards, many drivers were stuck on the roadways for long periods of time, even though they were close to their destinations.

If you run out of gas or your car breaks down on the highway, turn on your emergency flashers, signal to the right and try to get out of the moving traffic lanes. If there is a shoulder, pull the car as far onto it as possible, preferably beyond any curve in the road, while remaining on level ground. If you are able to get away from traffic, the safest thing to do is to stay in your car with the windows minimally open and the doors locked until help arrives. If you and your family decide to leave the car, exit on the passenger side and don't stand alongside, in front of or behind the car. Get as far away from the car as possible. Keep your hazard lights on during the daytime. Don't turn them on at night, because drivers behind you may think your car is still moving, albeit slowly. At night, keep the car's interior lights on.

If you're on a road without a shoulder and the engine still runs, keep driving until you can get off the road. If the car has a flat tire, proceed slowly—crawl!—until you reach a safe location, away from traffic. Don't drive fast on the rim because you don't want to generate sparks.

How to Stay Safe in an Automobile

Don't try to save the tire rim at the expense of your family's safety.

AAA advises that if you can't get your car to a location away from the traffic, or if you are unsure about your safety, don't stay in your car.

Open the car hood to make drivers aware that your car is disabled.

Tie a white or colored handkerchief, scarf or other material to the antenna or door handle or hold it in place by closing it in a window (if the window has power).

Place flares or warning triangles behind your car so drivers will know the car is disabled. AAA suggests that one flare or triangle be placed ten feet behind the side of the car closest to the road. Place the second one hundred feet directly behind the car, near the middle of the bumper. Place the third one hundred to three hundred feet behind the right side of the car. Watch out for oncoming traffic.

Don't try to make repairs to the car. Call 911 or other roadside assistance.

If you have a roadside assistance program, keep the number programmed into your cell phone or close at hand.

Never try to cross a highway on foot.

AAA offers many other tips on dealing with highway breakdowns. Check out their web sites.

How to be safe driving in the fog.

The best advice is to stay off the roads in heavy fog.

If you're already on the highway when fog rolls in, turn on your low beam lights or fog lights if you have them for better visibility. Bright lights reflect off the fog and make it difficult to see the road.

Drive slowly and keep your car window open a little so you can hear cars you might not see. Turn off the radio or any sound-producing devices. *Hazardous driving conditions require your undivided attention.*

Many newer vehicles have a button that will enhance one of the rear brake lights to allow the vehicle to be seen better during foggy situations. If your car has it, use it.

Use the white line down the right side of the road to guide you.

Don't tailgate and don't try to pass slow-moving vehicles.

Don't stop on the road or even on the shoulder.

If at all possible, exit the highway and find a place where you can be safe until the fog lifts, or, if you must continue driving, stay on service roads or streets and drive slowly.

How to be safe at the gas station.

The rise in the number of fires at gas pumps during refueling has lead professionals to conclude that many of them may be a result of static electricity. These incidents took place during extremely cold weather. Gasoline vapors, released during refueling, are highly combustible and easily ignited by a single spark. That spark can be created accidently by static electricity.

You know what it feels like when you've created static electricity at home. When you run across a carpeted floor and then touch something metal, you feel a shock, as if a jolt of electricity were going through you. That's *static electricity*. When you brush your hair in dry weather and your hair stands away from your head, that's also *static electricity*.

To reduce the threat of static electricity fires while you're pumping gasoline, *don't reenter the car while the gas is pumping*. Reentering the car can cause your body to build up static electricity from your clothes rubbing against the seat. When you touch the gas pump nozzle, you can transfer the static electricity to the fuel tank and ignite it. If you *must* reenter the car during refueling, as you get out, touch the outside metal part of the car door farthest from the pump to discharge the static electricity before you touch the gas pump nozzle. Under the same weather conditions, *before* you start pumping gas, it is advisable to touch the metal part of the car door to discharge the static electricity when you first get out. After refueling, touch the car far from the gas nozzle *before* putting the nozzle back into the pump.

Some states have enacted laws that prohibit locking clips at the end of the nozzle. A locking clip is the device that permits you to take your hand off the pump nozzle as it's filling your gas tank.

Other preventive measures.

Don't smoke at the gas station.

While there is no solid evidence that cell phones or other electronic gadgets cause explosions while you are refueling, it's better to be safe than sorry. Turn off cell phones and other electronic gadgets while you're pumping gas.

Filling portable fuel containers.

Never fill a gas can while it is inside a car trunk, van, or pickup bed or on any surface other than the ground. The plastic bed liner of a pickup truck or the carpet inside a car acts as an insulator and won't permit the static electricity from the flowing gasoline vapors to discharge. The static electricity will discharge into the grounded gas nozzle, potentially causing a spark that can ignite the gasoline. Accidents can occur whether you are using an ungrounded metal or plastic gas can.

The correct way to fill a gas can is to place it on the ground and fill it on the ground. This way the can is *grounded*, meaning there's a path for any electricity to discharge safely. When filling the can, keep it away from your car and those of other customers. Keep the nozzle in contact with the can while filling.

CHAPTER 5

How to Stay Safe at the Playground

IN THE READING ROOM

The apartment complex where Eddie's mom lives has an exciting and colorful playground with lots of play equipment, a picnic area, a sandbox, and a fountain. On Sunday afternoons, Dad comes early to pick up Eddie. He meets Mom and Eddie at the playground, where they spend a couple of hours before they leave for home.

The first time Mom took Eddie to the playground, she made sure it was safe and that the equipment was in good repair and appropriate for his age. Mom tells Eddie to play carefully and follow the rules. The following are some of the safety rules that Mom wants Eddie to know:

Playground Rules

- Stay where your parent or caregiver can see you at all times.
- Stay in the section of the playground set up for children your age.
- Wear closed, nonslip shoes or sneakers, not flip-flops or sandals.
- *Don't* wear loose clothing, scarves, drawstring sweatshirts, necklaces, purse straps, or anything that can catch on the rides.
- If you see older kids playing rough, kicking sand, or doing dangerous stunts, stay away from them. If they come into your area of the playground, tell your parent or caregiver.
- Don't use slides when it's very hot or when the equipment is wet and slippery.
- Be polite and respectful to other children and adults.

Accidents occur when you ignore safety rules. Always use playground equipment correctly.

How to Stay Safe at the Playground

Slides

- Before you get on the slide, make sure no one is in the way.
- Don't climb up the slide. Don't go down the slide lying on your back.
- When climbing the ladder, take one step at a time and always hold onto the handrail.
- Go down the slide feet first, sitting up.
- When you reach the bottom, make room for the next child.

Swings
- Use swings that are suitable for your size and age.
- Hold on with both hands.

- Tell anyone pushing you on the swing not to push you too high and not to push the swing in a twisting motion so it can't swing straight.
- Don't lean too far back or forward as you swing.
- Always sit on swings. Don't stand or kneel on them.
- Stand back from swings that are in motion.
- Only one child should go on a swing at a time.

Seesaws
- Never have more than one child on a seat.
- Make sure the child at the other end of the seesaw is about your size and weight.
- Face forward and hold the bar with two hands.
- Keep your feet out to the sides, not under the seesaw.
- Never stand on a seesaw or rock in the middle.
- Never climb on a seesaw while it's moving.
- Never jump off a seesaw when the other child is at the top.
- Stand back when others are using the seesaw.

Climbing rock walls or other climbing equipment
- Only climb on equipment that's right for your age and size.

- Don't try to climb if there are many children ahead of you.
- Use both hands and don't reach too high above you.
- Stay far behind the person in front of you.
- When you near the bottom as you come down the wall, drop down, knees bent, and land on both feet.
- Preschoolers should not climb above five feet.
- Stay away from monkey bars and horizontal ladders until you're old enough and strong enough to support yourself.
- If you use merry-go-rounds or other carousel type rides, make sure you hang on tight and are supervised by an adult.

Remember: stay safe and sound at the playground.

CHAPTER 6

How to Stay Safe Outdoors in the Summer

IN THE READING ROOM

Maria lives with Mami in a two-family home that they share with Maria's uncle and aunt and their children,

Pablo and Anna. Their house is on a treelined street in a beach community. Maria's aunt looks after her when Mami's at work as a nurse in the local hospital.

The children share a big old dog named Ruby who lives on the deck in a doghouse. In the summer, Ruby moves to a kennel in the shaded backyard.

During the summer Maria plays outdoors with her cousins and with Ruby. When she's at work, Mami worries about Maria and her cousins, so in the evening, she tells Maria the things she needs to know to stay safe outdoors. These are the things that Mami thinks are important:

As the weather heats up, swarms of insects will invade decks, porches, lawns, and gardens. They'll show up at the beach, park, and even on village, town, or city streets. Some insects are harmless (ladybugs). Others may be dangerous. Watch out for bees and wasps (including yellow jackets and hornets). These dangerous insects have one thing in common: they sting when they're disturbed. If you're stung, immediately tell an adult. Being stung will hurt but, with proper care, you'll be fine.

Sometimes a person can have an allergic reaction to a sting. If your skin turns red or swells where you were stung or if you have trouble breathing or are feeling dizzy, you may be having an allergic reaction. Tell an adult how you feel and have someone take you to the doctor or to a hospital emergency room for treatment.

If a bee, wasp, or hornet comes near you, don't swat at it. Stand still and wait for it to fly away.

- Don't wear sweet-smelling lotions, which attract bees.
- Wear long pants and long-sleeved shirts outdoors on the grass or in wooded areas. "This advice is not too helpful," Mami says, "when you're in the kiddie pool or running through water sprinklers."

Mosquitoes

Another annoying insect to avoid is the mosquito. Mosquitoes are around early in the morning and at sunset. Their bites can be painful and, when there is an allergic reaction, it can be dangerous. They are also carriers of the West Nile Virus which is particularly dangerous for small children. The CDC suggests that repellents containing up to 30 percent DEET offer the greatest protection against mosquitoes and ticks. They can be used on children over two months of age. Follow the directions on the package for proper application.

You and your family can help keep mosquitoes away by draining all standing water near your house: birdbaths, buckets, flowerpots, kiddie pools, etc. Frequently change your pet's water and the water in a birdbath.

"By the way," Mami says, "It's OK to swat mosquitoes."

Ticks

Two common types of ticks are dog and deer ticks.

Dog ticks are big enough to see on your dog's fur. Most of the time they're harmless, but they can cause Rocky Mountain spotted fever. Dogs should be bathed with a tick shampoo and should wear a tick collar.

Deer ticks are tiny and may carry Lyme Disease.

If you are bitten by a tick, you may not feel it at the time, but the area surrounding the bite may turn red. If you see signs of a tick (a tiny black dot on your skin) or redness from a tick bite, tell an adult right away.

To protect against tick bites when playing outdoors, wear long pants and a long-sleeved shirt. Tuck your pants legs into your socks. This is not a perfect solution, since ticks frequently find their way into your clothes and socks. Your parent may decide to spray a tick and insect spray on your clothing to reduce the likelihood of getting bit. Refer to the above section regarding mosquito repellants.

When you come in from the outside, have an adult check your body from head to toe. Examine any place that retains moisture, such as under your arms, your waist, the back of your knees, etc. If a tick is found, your parent or caregiver should remove it carefully with a pair of tweezers by grasping the tick near the surface of your skin and using light pressure. If the whole tick is not removed, your parent should contact your doctor.

Just as I was about to submit my finished manuscript for publication, a situation occurred which I had never considered, and I felt compelled to add it to this chapter.

My son David and five-year-old granddaughter Ilana returned from a day trip to the resort town of Montauk, Long Island and recounted an experience they had earlier that evening. It was sundown and they were getting ready to come home when they encountered a young girl who was screaming hysterically and writhing in pain. She was accompanied by two other teenage girls and her mother. The street was jam-packed with tourists, but no one was coming to the girl's aid. She sobbed that something had crawled into her ear, causing excruciating pain.

David has a habit of keeping a spray bottle of water handy. He grabbed the bottle and a flashlight, tilted the girl's head to the side and sprayed the water into her ear. When the ear canal filled, he tilted her head down to allow the water to run out, and sure enough, the bug crawled out. The girl's mother knocked the bug out of her daughter's ear. The pain subsided and the girl calmed down. David's preparedness and quick response saved the day. My granddaughter remained calm, signaling to passersby, that an emergency was occurring.

Insect in the ear.

I researched the subject of ear emergencies and found a number of websites dealing with the topic of *insect in the ear.* **The following recommendations are *not* applicable to children who have tubes in their ears or a history of ear problems. In those instances, call the child's doctor immediately.**

The National Institutes of Health, Medline Plus, recommends the following.

- Don't put a finger in the ear, because this may make the insect sting.

How to Stay Safe Outdoors in the Summer

- Turn the child's head to the side where the insect crawled in and wait to see if the insect crawls or flies out.
- If this fails, pour mineral, olive or baby oil into the ear. As you pour the oil, pull the ear lobe gently backward and upward for an adult, or backward and downward for a child. The insect should suffocate and may float out in the oil. The Mayo Clinic website mayoclinic.com suggests:

- Don't probe the ear with a cotton swab, matchstick or any other tool.
- Try using gravity by tilting the head to the affected side to try to dislodge the object.
- For insects, they also recommend using oil.

A website pohick.blogspot.com advises the following:

- Don't try to remove an insect with tweezers, cotton swabs or other objects. This can lodge the insect deeper into the ear canal.
- Using same position, fill the ear with oils as above. If you don't have oil, flush the ear with warm water allowing it to overflow. Watch for the insect to be flushed out.

The Boston Children's Hospital website also recommends using oil to suffocate the insect and if the insect doesn't come out, pour a small amount of warm water into the ear canal to flush it out.

In any event, the best advice is to seek medical assistance as quickly as possible. The ear canal is very sensitive.

Woodland creatures.

Maria's neighborhood has lots of woodland creatures roaming around. When she wakes up in the morning, dozens of wild turkeys parade across her lawn. Rabbits hop about and deer families gather near the house to nibble on the shrubs and plants. Lots of smaller creatures burrow beneath the ground, scamper about, or creepy crawl under wood piles. Big blue birds, medium-sized red birds, and lots of small brown birds come up on the deck to eat the dog's food.

Stay away from outdoor creatures. Don't play with, feed, or touch animals and birds, except your pets, of course. That includes squirrels, moles, bats, raccoons, skunks, snakes, mice, and other outdoor creatures.

These animals are afraid of people. If you get too close and frighten them, they may bite or scratch you. Some may carry rabies, a serious disease. If you are scratched or bitten, don't wait. Tell your parent or caregiver immediately, and try to identify what animal bit you. You may need medical help.

Sometimes, a lost or homeless dog or cat will wander around your neighborhood. They are called *strays*. Never go near or pet a stray animal. Don't pet any dogs or cats, even if you know their owners, unless the owner is there and gives you permission.

The Humane Society of the United States recommends that even before you pet your own dog, you should let him see and sniff you first. The society advises you to be aware of the body signals a dog gives off when he is about to bite:

- Tensed body
- Stiff tail
- Pulled back head and/or ears
- Furrowed brow
- Eyes rolled so the whites are visible
- Yawning (Purpose: to show you his teeth)
- Flicking tongue

If a strange dog comes toward you, don't run. It will think it's a game and will chase you. Stand still with your hands by your sides while it sniffs you. Avoid eye contact. When the dog starts to lose interest in you, slowly back away.

If the dog attacks, the Humane Society recommends "that you 'feed' him your jacket, purse, bicycle, or anything that you can put between yourself and the dog."

In the July 9, 2013 edition of the Wall Street Journal, dog trainer Victoria Stillwell advised that "if a dog is on a child and you're pulling it off, you're making the wound on that child deeper". She suggests putting a coat or T-shirt over the dog's head. She says, "When dogs can't see, they panic and open their mouths."

If a dog keeps annoying you whenever you go outside, your parent should speak to the dog's owner about not letting the dog loose when children are outdoors. If the dog is a stray, your parent should call the local dog catcher or the police.

Remember: stay safe in the sun and you'll have lots of fun.

CHAPTER 7

How to Stay Safe in the Water

IMPORTANT INFORMATION FOR THE PARENT, GRANDPARENT, OR OTHER CAREGIVER

What you should know before your child goes in the water.

Weather Conditions.

Whether you're at the ocean, lake, pond, pool, hot tub, water park, resort, or other water destination, before you go into the water, the first thing you should consider is the weather. Most people get the weather news from their local television stations, radio reports, Internet weather sites, newspapers, etc. Some people own NOAA (National Oceanic and Atmospheric Administration) radios, which are on all the time and sound alarms and broadcast weather warnings. The NOAA radio is an early-warning system in your home. *The National Weather Service also broadcasts information about rip currents, which can be found on NOAA Weather Radio and on the Internet.*

The National Weather Service uses the words *watches* and *warnings* to tell you about potentially bad weather coming your way. A *watch* means it's likely you'll be getting bad weather soon, but it's not near you yet. It tells you to watch out for it. Sometimes, a storm comes so fast, there is no time for a further *warning*. If your neighborhood is experiencing a *weather watch*, keep your family out of the water.

A *warning* lets you know that the bad weather is right where you are. It tells you the type of weather condition you are encountering, such as heavy rain and fog, thunderstorms, lightning strikes, tropical storms, hurricanes, tornadoes, nor'easters, flash floods, etc.

While the weather is bad, stay out of the water. Once you determine that the weather is clear, you're good to go.

IN THE READING ROOM

Maria, Pablo, and Anna learned to swim at an early age. By the time they were five, they could float on their backs, dog paddle, and swim across a pool. But even with these skills, Mami worries about their safety. She works in a hospital and knows how dangerous water can be because adults and children who nearly drowned come into the emergency room on a regular basis during warm weather. Mami says there are so many water-related issues to be concerned about that she arranged them by type of danger. Some of the rules directly apply to you. Others apply to the person watching you, and the rest apply to the people who own or operate the pool, spa, or other water facility.

Mami says, "If the weather is bad, don't go in the water. The warning applies to the pool, hot tub, ocean, or any other body of water. It applies to swimming or boating."

Keeping safe at the pool.

Drowning is the leading cause of injury-related death among children between one and four years old and the third leading cause of death among children generally.

- The person watching you while you're in the pool should have a cell phone in case of emergency and should pay *undivided* attention to you. *Most drowning deaths occur when a caregiver is with you, but is not paying full attention.* That means your caregiver should not be reading, checking

e-mail, texting, etc. *as long as you are in the pool* or, for that matter, any other body of water.
- Don't play or swim in a pool, even your own, without adult supervision. Never swim alone. Always swim with a buddy or an adult.
- Take swimming lessons early on and learn water safety skills.
- If you can't swim or are a beginner, wear a life jacket and stay at the shallow end of the pool unless an adult is swimming with you.
- Keep away from pool drains or other openings. Your hair can be sucked into the drains and pull you under the water.
- Stay in the shade as much as possible. When you're out of the water, cover up and wear a hat and sunglasses. Apply sunscreen 30 minutes before exposure to the sun. Make sure you apply the sunscreen to your ears, nose, lips and feet as well as to all the exposed parts of your body. Reapply every two hours after coming out of the water or after excessive sweating.
- Don't run, play rough, push, or splash other children in or around the pool.
- *Never* dive into above-ground pools. Don't dive into in-ground pools, unless a lifeguard or

knowledgeable adult tells you the water is deep enough for diving. Then, only dive off a diving board. Diving off the side of a pool or into shallow water can kill you or cause permanent, devastating injuries.
- Never chew gum while swimming or playing in the water.

Remember: be cool! Follow the rules and enjoy the pool.

How do you know if someone is drowning?

There are excellent web sites and blogs which explain what signs to look for.

Drowning is not the ferocious splashing and calling for help that most of us learned to expect from watching movies and television. It is a silent event. Half the children who will drown next year will be within twenty-five yards of a parent or other adult. It is vital to learn the signs of drowning.

Keeping safe at the ocean.

The ocean is beautiful, refreshing, and delightful on hot summer days, but it can be dangerous, even for good swimmers. *To stay safe in the ocean, follow these rules:*

- Learn to read the warning signs at the beach that tell you when to stay out of the water and whether the beach has a lifeguard at the time you're there.
- Never go into the ocean unless a lifeguard is present. Obey all orders from lifeguards.
- Unless you're a very good swimmer, wear a life jacket in the water. Don't rely on blow-up rafts or other blow-up toys to keep you safe in the ocean because they can lose air or float away from you.
- Before you go into the ocean, test the water temperature to make sure it's not too cold.
- If the waves get big and rough, get out of the water. Don't stand with your back to the waves. Big ones can knock you over.
- Swim close to the shore, following the shore line.
- Make sure your feet can touch the ground and wear something to protect your feet from the rough ocean floor.
- Stay far away from rocks, piers, jetties, and pilings. If you trip or if a wave pushes you against them, you can get cut or bruised.
- Don't play rough in the ocean or dunk anyone under water.
- Avoid swallowing ocean water.

- Learn about rip currents and what to do if you get caught in one.

Remember: no lifeguard, no swimming.

IMPORTANT INFORMATION FOR THE PARENT, GRANDPARENT, OR OTHER CAREGIVER

Recently, the NOAA-USLA Rip Current Task Force advised that water-related deaths from rip currents come in second after heat-related deaths and ahead of deaths from floods, tornadoes, lightning, and hurricanes.

The following is a brief explanation of tides and rip currents.

What is a tide?

A tide is the rise and fall of the ocean, usually occurring twice a day. We talk about *high* tides and *low* tides. In a *high* tide, the ocean rises as it comes toward the shore. In a *low* tide, the ocean recedes, flowing away from the shore out to sea. When the tide comes in, it loses energy as it reaches the gentle upward slope of the shore, and when it flows back out, it's generally with minimum force and *spread over a wide area.*

A rip current happens when the *outgoing* tide gets concentrated into a narrow opening or channel, changing the dynamic of the flow and increasing its force. Unwary swimmers and waders can be caught in a rip current while standing in shallow water.

How does this happen?

At high tide, you can't see if anything unusual or dangerous is lurking under the ocean near the shoreline. Sometimes *sandbars* (ridges of sand under the ocean along the shore) are formed. Sandbars block the tide from flowing out to sea. When the outgoing tide gathers enough momentum to break the sandbar apart, it creates a channel through which the tide can flow in and out. The rush of water through the channel is so concentrated, swift, and forceful (like water from a bathtub pouring down the drain), it can carry a person in its path out to sea. This is a rip current.

What to do if you get caught in a rip current.

- Stay calm. You can get through it if you understand what is happening.
- First, draw attention to yourself by screaming and waving your arms so that people on the beach or near you in the water will know you're in trouble.
- Don't try to swim toward shore *against* the rip current, because the force of the water pushing you away is too strong and you'll get worn out in moments. It will wear out even an excellent swimmer.
- Tread water or float on your back with your hands spread out to the side. If you're a good swimmer, swim or float parallel to the shoreline as much as possible.
- Once you are through the channel, you should be able to swim at an angle toward shore.
- Try to keep your nose and mouth above water.

- Some beaches are known to have *frequent* rip currents. If your beach is one of them, *find another beach where your child can swim safely.*

How to help someone who is caught in a rip current.

Frequently, well-intentioned individuals who attempt to rescue someone caught in a rip current become drowning victims themselves. If you can, yell instructions to the victim, telling him how to escape the rip current. Alert a lifeguard and others in the water and on the beach to the situation. If you can do it safely, throw a floating device to the person.

How to stay safe in a pool.

According to recently published reports, the number one cause of toddler deaths is *accidental* drowning. It takes only a few inches of water for a child to drown.

For those of you who have an in-ground pool at home, this section addresses key elements of pool safety. Most of these measures also pertain to above-ground pools, hot tubs, spas, and whirlpools.

In-ground home pools present a real and present danger to children.

Pool Fencing.

Your pool should be *fenced* on all *four* sides. In the case of an in-ground pool that sits directly behind your house, *the fourth side of the fence should be between your house and the pool.* The fence must be tall enough to stop young children from climbing over it. It should be at least four feet high. Contact your local municipality for code and zoning requirements. It shouldn't have anything on it that could provide a hand or foothold. Preferably, it should not be made of chain link, which is easy for a child to climb, unless the links are small enough to prevent getting a hand-or foothold. If the fence is slatted, the slats (boards, bars) should be close together and made of a rigid material that can't be pried apart by a resourceful child. The fence gate should be self-closing and self-latching with a lock mounted out of a child's reach. Preferably, the lock should require a key to open.

Children are inventive. They'll use whatever they can to get over the fence. Never store climbable items near the fence (chairs, tables, etc.). Never store trash or other containers near the fence, which can be used as step stools to access the pool. Never store pool chemicals near the pool. Besides being used as step stools, the chemicals are dangerous and should be stored in an inaccessible, locked storage area.

Other safety tips.

Remove shrubs, trees, hedges, etc. blocking your view of the pool from the house.

How to Stay Safe in the Water

It only takes a moment for a child to drown in a pool. *You can't have too many safeguards to protect your child or your neighbors' children from drowning or from severe and permanent injury.* Even with all the safeguards in place, *a child should never be in a pool without constant supervision.*

Pool Alarm Systems:

There are numerous alarm systems on the market. Before purchasing one, find out if the system you've chosen has been evaluated by an independent rating organization. *None of the alarms are foolproof.* For example, the *surface wave detection alarm* system will sound when the surface of the water in the pool is disturbed, such as when a child falls or jumps into the pool. But it may not activate if a child climbs down the steps at the shallow end of the pool and enters the water without disturbing it. While the surface wave detection alarm may not detect the presence of the child, it can be set off by wind, heavy rain, or falling debris. Keep in mind that the alarm has to be removed when anyone is swimming.

Another type of alarm system is the *subsurface wave detection alarm system,* which has sensors below the surface of the water that react to wave-caused changes in pressure.

The *personal immersion detector wristband alarm system* is a third type of warning device. In this case, the child wears a wristband with a sensor, which causes an alarm to go off when it is immersed in water. The system has a base station in the house where the alarm sounds. You must remember to remove the wristband when the child is actually allowed in the water.

It is highly recommended that door and window alarms be installed in your house as well as pool-gate alarms, but none of these safety devices can substitute for the undivided attention of the parent, caregiver, guardian, etc. Again, contact your local municipality for applicable regulations.

Install drain covers to keep children from getting caught by the strong suction power in big pools.

Install safety ropes to divide the shallow and deep sections of the pool.

Install a slip resistant product on concrete walks surrounding the pool.

Keep life preservers and a *shepherd's hook* handy at poolside. A shepherd's hook is a long pole with a curved hook on the end. Its purpose is to grasp a swimmer in trouble. The swimmer can grab the hook or, if unconscious, the hook is flexible enough to be wrapped around the waist or backside. Never use the hook to pull a person by the neck. Using a shepherd's hook requires practice. The rescuer should stand away from the edge of the pool to avoid being pulled into the pool by the drowning person.

Never leave a pool cover partially on when children are in the pool. They can get trapped under the cover.

How to Stay Safe in the Water

Don't keep blow-up pool toys around when not in use. Don't keep riding toys near the pool. Certainly don't keep electric appliances near the pool.

If a child falls into your pool, scream for help. Get the child out of the pool and place him or her on the pool deck. Check to see if he or she is conscious. According to the Red Cross, if someone is with you, have the person call 911 at once. If the child is not breathing normally, start CPR and don't stop until emergency help comes. If you're alone in the same situation, begin CPR and then call 911. Continue CPR until help comes. Chapter 13 provides some CPR guidelines.

Hot Tubs, Spas, Whirlpools.

Whether at home, at a hotel, or visiting a neighbor, family member, or friend with a hot tub, spa, or whirlpool, don't let your child go in or near it without adult supervision. A hot tub, spa, or whirlpool can be relaxing and enjoyable for adults, but can be *deadly* for young children.

The water may be too hot for a young child's sensitive skin, and the child can suffer heatstroke or skin burns. Children with long hair can drown if their hair is sucked into the drain and they are pulled down and held under water.

Even adults with long hair should not put their heads under water. Most of the safety bells and whistles in the pool section apply to hot tubs, spas, and whirlpools.

Spas should have lockable safety covers to prevent access.

IN THE READING ROOM

How to stay safe in an inflatable boat:

- It's best to take swimming lessons and learn about water safety *before* you go boating.
- If the weather is bad, don't go out in a boat.
- *Always wear a Coast Guard approved life jacket.* Make sure it fits well and is put on properly. Put the life jacket on *before* you get in the boat.
- Be careful getting into the boat. Accidents frequently occur when people are trying to get in boats from launch areas.
- Standing up in an inflatable boat while it's moving can be dangerous. When you get into the boat, immediately take a seat.
- Never take a boat out without an adult present. The adult should be a good swimmer and should be wearing a life jacket as well.
- The boat should be sailed near the shoreline.

Remember: follow safety rules in a boat and you'll stay afloat.

Water Park Safety

How to Stay Safe in the Water

IMPORTANT INFORMATION FOR THE PARENT, GRANDPARENT, OR OTHER CAREGIVER

Water parks are tons of fun, but they can be dangerous

- Remind your child of stranger danger. Point out trustworthy adults. Have a designated place to meet if you get separated. If the child is old enough, give him a cell phone with your numbers programmed. *Please, no fancy phones which are targets for thieves.*
- Dress your child in easily recognizable clothing for simple identification if you need to report your lost child to park authorities. Keep up-to-date photos of your children with you.
- Bring sunscreen, bug spray, hand wipes, bandages, sun hats, sunglasses and plenty of water.
- For very young children, bring a stroller.
- Make sure your child is wearing comfortable shoes, not sandals, or flip flops. Consider water shoes which have rubber soles.
- Read the sign for each ride before you let your child go on. Check to see if there is a lifeguard at each ride.
- Make sure your child is tall enough, old enough, and healthy enough for the particular ride. This rule applies to rides that are not water-related, such as carnival and resort rides. Even if your child meets the park's requirements, as a parent, use your judgment as to whether your child is self-controlled enough for the particular ride.

- Teach your child to stay seated and keep his arms and legs inside the car. If the ride has seat belts or safety bars, they should be used. Tell your child to stay seated until told by the ride operator that it's safe to get off.
- Don't let your child wear long necklaces, straps, or anything that could get caught in equipment. If your child has long hair, keep it in a hairstyle that will prevent it from getting caught.

Part II

Dangers in the Home

CHAPTER 8

How to Avoid Accidents at Home

IMPORTANT INFORMATION FOR THE PARENT, GRANDPARENT, OR OTHER CAREGIVER

We use the word *accident* all the time. Your child spills a glass of milk while eating dinner and tells you, "Oops! It was an accident!" Or knocks over a lamp while playing tag with a sibling and cries, "It was an accident!" In the first instance, the child was eating nicely and tipped the glass over and spilled the milk. That *was* an accident. In the second example, despite being told a hundred times not to run in the living room, the child disobeyed you and knocked over the lamp. Is that really an accident?

An accident is something that causes damage or harm and happens *without warning* and *not* on purpose. Although an accident is not caused on purpose, it can be the consequence of careless behavior (such as the lamp being knocked over), a lack of understanding of the danger involved (playing with matches), or failure to take protective steps to prevent it from happening (leaving poisonous chemicals where your child can get them).

Accidents can happen anywhere and everywhere. Teach your child how to avoid them.

IN THE READING ROOM

Jack and Jillian and their parents, Dr. and Mrs. Smith, live in a big old house on a narrow street in a tiny village of a large town. Jillian is starting high school and Jack is entering kindergarten. Their father is a pediatrician (children's doctor) who has an office in their house. Their mother teaches ballet to young children in the afternoon at a nearby studio. When she's away from the house, Jack plays in the healthy children's waiting room until his mother or his sister gets home.

Dr. Smith takes care of lots of children. He gives them shots, weighs them, and measures their height, and when they are sick, he prescribes medicine to make them well. What bothers him is when a child is brought to see him as a result of an accident that he knows could have been avoided with good sense and caution on the part of the child's parent.

How to Avoid Accidents at Home

Jack is lucky to have three people to guide and protect him: his father, his mother, and his older sister. Dr. Smith makes sure that *everything* in the house is in good condition and *nothing* dangerous is lurking about. His mother teaches him the dos and don'ts of safety, and his sister makes sure Jack follows the rules when she's watching him while their mother is at the studio.

Jack wants you to learn what Dr. Smith does to keep his family safe. He wants you to recognize potential dangers and avoid them.

This section addresses the roles of both the parent and child.

How to prevent accidents.

In the kitchen.

Child:

- Never touch pots or pans on the stove without adult supervision. If a pot handle is sticking out in front of the stove, ask an adult to turn the handle around.
- Don't stand near the stove when something is cooking or baking.

- Don't use a microwave by yourself. Have an adult microwave for you.
- Don't climb on countertops to try to reach things in cabinets.

Parent:

- Don't leave cabinet drawers open. They are at a child's eye level.
- In order for a fire to start, a heat source, combustible material (fuel) and oxygen must be present. Removing one of the three will either prevent a fire or stop an existing one.
- Cooking fires are widespread and often the result of leaving the stove unattended while food is cooking. The most common sources of stove fires are grease, oils, and *flammable* materials (items which can catch fire). Make sure towels, pot holders, and other flammable items are kept away from the stove.
- Clean the stove and oven to prevent grease buildup.
- If a fire starts in a frying pan, turn off the stove and cover the pan with a lid. By doing this you

eliminate the oxygen feeding the fire. You can buy small *fire blankets*, which can be used to put out kitchen fires. They can be more useful than a fire extinguisher because they are easier and quicker to use. Carefully place the *fire blanket* over the pan to smother the flames. These *fire blankets* can smother barbeque flare-ups as well.
- Never try to put out a grease fire with water.
- If a fire starts in a toaster oven, close the door to the oven and unplug. Cover with a *fire blanket* if you have one.
- Don't wear loose-fitting clothes or loose sleeves while cooking.

In the bathroom.

Parent:

- Keep hair blowers, electric curling irons or straighteners, electric razors, etc. away from sinks, tubs, and showers. Keep them unplugged when not in use. Don't allow your young child to plug or unplug the appliance.

Child:

- Never put an electric appliance in or near water.

Parent:

- If you have an electric space heater in the bathroom, keep it a safe distance from the bathtub or shower.

In the laundry room.

Child:

- Help your parent with the laundry by taking the lint out of the lint filter in the dryer after a load of laundry is dried. The lint filter should be cleaned after *every* dryer load.

Parent:

- Check the dryer exhaust hose several times a year to make sure it's free of lint buildup.

How to Avoid Accidents at Home

Lint can accumulate and a spark can set it on fire.
- Check the outside dryer vent to make sure it's free of lint and that it opens and closes properly when the dryer is operating.
- Never store combustible items (products that can explode or burn) in the laundry room.

In the garage.

Parent:

- Lock up all cleaning products, chemicals and other poisonous items.

- Keep tools, hardware, wires, cords, rope, etc. out of reach of young children.

Child:

- If the garage is part of your house, make sure your parent teaches you how to open the garage door in case of an emergency. The garage offers a means of escape in case of fire.

In the bedroom.

Parent:

- Especially in a child's bedroom, don't place furniture in front of a window, which might have to be used as an escape route in the event of a fire.
- Make sure your child wears snug pajamas to bed. You may want to consider keeping a fire blanket within reach of your child's bed. If your child's clothing catches on fire, tightly wrap the blanket around the child and roll him on the floor to put out the fire.

General rules.

Child:
- Don't play with matches, lighters, or candles.
- Don't stand close to a fireplace or wood-burning stove when it's in use or when it's cooling down. Your clothes can catch on fire or you can get burned by flying sparks.

Parent:
- Have the fireplace chimney or wood-burning stove vent pipe cleaned and inspected regularly, especially if used frequently.
- Keep a fire screen in front of the fireplace to keep sparks from flying out.
- Never keep a rug in front of the fireplace or wood-burning stove.

Child:
- Don't keep toys or other items on the fireplace *hearth* (flat stones at the base of the fireplace).
- Keep pets away from the fireplace.

Parent:

- Make sure the fire in a fireplace or wood-burning stove is out before going to bed or leaving the house. Don't remove ashes or embers until they're *cold*. Once cold, they should be placed in a fireproof metal container and stored far away from the house.

Child:

- Don't touch space heaters or place items on them or near them.

Parent:

- Unplug the heater when you leave the room.
- Use a *heavy duty* extension cord to plug in an appliance (electric grill, etc.). The standard cords are not heavy enough to carry the electricity load of the appliance and can short, causing a fire. *Always* unplug the cord when you've finished using the appliance.

Remember: parents and children working together each day will keep the family out of harm's way.

CHAPTER 9

Additional Ways to Avoid Injuries at Home

IN THE READING ROOM

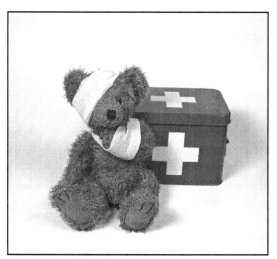

Mrs. Smith knows that accidents can happen even when parents are home. Each evening when the family settles down before going to bed, she takes time to go over additional safety rules with Jack. If Jillian is finished with her homework, she'll sometimes join Jack in the living room to listen. Now that Jillian is older, she thinks these rules seem so clear and straightforward that you wouldn't have to explain them. Of course, that's never the case.

Jack and Jillian want you to learn them as well.

- When walking down a flight of stairs, take one step at a time. Keep your eyes forward. Keep your hand closest to the banister free so you can hold on. Don't carry a lot of things. Don't carry a blanket or other long items that can trip you. Don't play on the steps or run down the stairs.
- Open doors slowly in case someone is standing behind the door. When closing the door, keep your hands and feet away from the door jambs.
- Never lock yourself into a room or lock a parent or caregiver out.
- Never run near sliding glass doors.
- Don't walk or run barefoot or in your socks on a slippery floor. Wear shoes, sneakers or slippers with grips on the bottom.
- Don't run on wet floors.
- If something spills, make sure it gets wiped up to prevent falls.
- Don't run in areas where there are loose rugs.
- Never run or jump around while chewing food, gum, or hard candy.

Additional Ways to Avoid Injuries at Home

- If a glass or dish breaks, call your parent or caregiver immediately. Don't try to clean up the broken pieces on your own.
- If you're bleeding from a scratch or cut, tell someone and apply first aid. Press on the scratch or cut, using a clean wash cloth to stop the bleeding. Then wash the area with warm water and mild soap, dry it, and place a bandage on it to keep it clean. If the bandage gets dirty or wet, change it.
- If the bleeding still doesn't stop or a sliver of glass remains in the cut, have someone take you to the doctor or the emergency room of the nearest hospital.

The following is a list of things you should never *do if you want to be safe:*

- Don't tilt your chair back when you're sitting at the table.
- Don't climb on a wall unit or shelves to reach for something.
- Don't climb into a clothes washer, dryer, refrigerator, toy box, or other space where you might not be able to get out.
- Don't play with cords on window blinds or shades.

- When playing, don't put things around your neck that can get caught on something.
- Don't put anything in your mouth that isn't food. That includes vitamins, pills, or medicine, unless specifically given to you by your parent. That also includes tiny toys, toy parts, magnets, beads, pebbles, balloons, plastic bags, or any other foreign (nonfood) objects.

CHAPTER 10

How to Stay Safe in Case of a Fire

IMPORTANT INFORMATION FOR THE PARENT, GRANDPARENT, OR OTHER CAREGIVER

I think this is the most difficult chapter to write, because so much depends on the type of home you live in, the layout of the rooms and exits, and whether the house is a one-, two- or three-story dwelling. If your family lives in a high-rise apartment building, there are other issues to deal with, such as having only one way out of the apartment, the danger of using an elevator during a fire, and how to know the location of a fire: on your floor or above or below your apartment. When do you stay in your apartment? When do you leave? When should you open a window and when shouldn't you?

The information in this chapter, like the others, is a non-professional interpretation of the numerous articles and documents on the Internet, in magazines, and in newspapers. It's a guide but should not be substituted for professional advice and instruction.

A fire in your home can be deadly. It could be triggered by an unpredictable event, such as a lightning strike. More times than not, it's caused by unawareness, carelessness, or a lack of preparedness.

When you live in an apartment building, you have little or no control over how the building is maintained. You have to rely on building management to do the right thing when it comes to fire safety. In an apartment building, a fire in someone else's apartment or in a public area can directly affect your family's safety. While many of the safety rules we've talked about in earlier chapters are indispensable in preventing a fire, most of them apply to single-family homes. High-rise apartment safety is another matter. Let's consider the safety issues in high-rise apartment buildings first.

Review your building's evacuation plan, which is generally posted in the lobby or other public area. Know the location of exit stairs and fire alarm pull stations. Be able to identify the sound of the building's fire alarm.

Never assume that someone else has called 911 or the fire department. Make the call.

If your apartment is in a *fireproof building,* you can still have fires in the building or in your apartment. The contents of your apartment can burn, throwing off tremendous heat, smoke, and harmful fumes. What *fireproof* means is that fire and smoke are more likely to be contained within an apartment itself. In a fireproof building, it's usually safer to stay in your apartment, unless that's where the fire is. If the fire is not in your apartment and you choose to leave, first touch your front door with the back of your hand. If the door feels warm, don't open it. Stay where you are. Fill the space around the door with wet towels or rags, or seal it with duct tape. Cover any vents to keep smoke out. Turn off air conditioners. With the many types of windows in today's apartment, it is difficult to advise you whether to open the windows or not. Much depends on whether the fire is above or below your apartment. *Ask your building manager or superintendent whether you should open windows in the event of a fire, and under what conditions.*

If you're *not* in immediate danger and you choose to stay in your apartment to wait for help, make sure the firefighters and management know you're there. If you choose to exit your apartment because there is no smoke or fire on your floor, follow your building's evacuation plan. Close all the doors in your apartment as you leave. If you don't hear the fire alarm, alert your neighbors by pulling the nearest pull-station alarm on your floor as you exit.

- *Never use the elevator*! Take the stairs. If you feel heat or smell smoke coming from below, don't proceed. If

the smoke gets heavy, stay low. Go back to a safe floor or to your apartment. *Don't go to the roof.*
- Check your smoke detectors regularly.
- Keep duct tape and flashlights handy.

In an apartment building, fire safety is in the hands of building management. In your own home, for the most part, you control the situation. Fire safety is in your hands.

Follow these essential steps to *prevent* or *survive* a fire.

- Conduct an inspection of your home for potential fire hazards.
- If you have not done so already, install battery-operated smoke and carbon monoxide detectors on each floor of your house, especially near bedrooms.
- Change the batteries in the smoke detectors and carbon monoxide detectors twice a year or more frequently. Even if you have hard-wired smoke and carbon monoxide detectors, install additional battery-operated units in case the electricity goes off and the battery backup fails. Keep the alarms dust free.
- A significant number of fires occur each heating season when bedding, drapes, rugs, and other flammable materials come in contact with baseboard or portable space heaters. Never put anything close to a heater. Don't use an extension cord with a space heater. Make sure you shut off the heater when you leave the room or go to bed.

How to Stay Safe in Case of a Fire

- Refrain from using halogen lamps in close proximity to any flammable material (drapes, furniture, books, etc. The extreme heat of halogen bulbs will cause a fire when any flammable material touches the bulb.

IN THE READING ROOM

What is a smoke detector (smoke alarm)?

A smoke detector is an important piece of equipment in your home. A smoke detector (alarm) is a device with a sensor and a horn. When it senses smoke, it will sound the horn to wake up your family and pets. It warns you about a fire even when you can't see the fire or smoke.

What to do in case the alarm goes off or you see smoke or fire.

If an alarm goes off or if you see smoke or fire, call out to your family members to warn them.

Get out of the house as fast as you can. Once you're outside the house, either you or your parent or caregiver should call 911 immediately. Use a cell phone or a neighbor's phone. Tell the operator that your house is on fire. Tell the operator your address, how many people are at home, and, if you can, where they are located in the house. Don't hang up until you are told to do so.

Never go back into the house. When the firefighters arrive, tell them if any people or pets are still inside.

Your parents should make a family escape plan. Practice escape routes from each room with them. Arrange a gathering place in advance so you know where to meet once you're out of the house. Have a backup place if, for some reason, the first one is unavailable.

If you can't get out quickly, call 911 from the house. Let the emergency operator know which rooms you and other family members are in. If you can, open a window and scream.

Never hide from firefighters or others trying to rescue you. Keep calling so they can find you.

If a door is closed on your escape route, check to see if smoke is coming under the door. If you see smoke, don't open the door. If you don't see smoke, touch the door with the back of your hand. If it's hot, don't open it. If possible, use another way out including a door or window.

According to the website Kids Health.org from the Nemours Foundation, if the doorknob is hot, don't open the door. If the doorknob is *not* hot and you don't see smoke, you can open the door slowly. If you suddenly feel heat or see smoke, quickly close the door. If you can't get out right away, block spaces around the door with whatever you can (sheets, blankets, clothing) to keep heat and smoke from coming in under or around the door. If there is no heat or smoke, go to your escape route exit.

In a heavy smoke situation, stay close to the floor. Crawl on your hands and knees under the smoke to the nearest exit. Cover your nose and mouth. If you can get to water quickly, wet a towel, T-shirt, rag, or any other item, and hold it over your nose and mouth.

If your clothes are on fire, don't run! *Stop, drop, and roll. Cover your eyes and face.* Wrap yourself in a fire blanket if you have one or a towel, regular blanket, or rug to put out the flames.

Remember: give fire prevention all your attention.

CHAPTER 11

How to Prevent Carbon Monoxide Poisoning

IMPORTANT INFORMATION FOR THE PARENT, GRANDPARENT, OR OTHER CAREGIVER

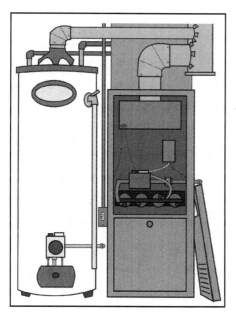

This chapter is primarily for the reader. Your child plays a minimal role here. Where your child needs to know something, I mention it.

Many home appliances operate on natural gas, including furnaces, hot water heaters, stoves, clothes dryers, and gas grills. One of the most important things you can do to keep your family safe is to install carbon-monoxide detectors on each floor. Carbon monoxide detectors are an early warning system that senses the poisonous fumes given off by a defective appliance, clogged vent, gas leak or other source and alerts you to the problem.

What causes a buildup of carbon monoxide?

If a gas-operated appliance malfunctions or is not vented correctly, natural gas can't burn completely. The incomplete burning process produces an odorless, colorless, tasteless, poisonous gas called carbon monoxide (CO). Carbon Monoxide can kill. Because the gas is so dangerous and there was no way to detect it, gas service companies added a chemical to it that makes the gas smell like rotten eggs to let you know when there is a gas leak in your house.

A carbon monoxide detector is a device that recognizes and measures the CO gas concentration in the air. When it detects CO, it sets off an alarm.

Explain to your child about CO detectors and what to do if the alarm sounds.

Tell your child to immediately yell out to family members to get out of the house if the carbon monoxide detector alarm goes off. Make sure your child can distinguish between the sounds of the smoke alarm and the CO detector.

Make sure your child understands never to go back into the house until the gas company professional responders say that it's safe to reenter. *Call 911 from outside the house.*

How to Prevent Carbon Monoxide Poisoning

What are the symptoms of carbon monoxide poisoning?

Headache, nausea, chest pain, dizziness, and a feeling of confusion are some of the symptoms. As the level of CO increases, symptoms become more severe and can include unconsciousness.

To reduce the risk of carbon monoxide poisoning, do the following:

- Make sure your furnace, water heater, and other oil or gas burning equipment are installed correctly and serviced regularly.
- A bird's nest, leaves, or soot can block a chimney or vent pipe, forcing CO fumes to vent back into your home. Cracked masonry can have the same effect. Have the flue cleaned regularly and make sure the chimney has an adequate draft.
- Wood-burning or gas fireplaces can also cause a CO buildup. Keep a window slightly open to allow circulation of fresh air when the fireplace or wood-burning stove is in operation.
- Make sure all gas appliances are vented to the outside of the house to prevent CO buildup.

Sometimes, particularly in the winter during a power outage, people take risky steps to stay warm, such as use their gas stoves for heat. These desperate measures can result in more dangerous consequences than just the loss of heat.

Never do any of the following:

- Never use your gas stove to heat the house.
- Never use a charcoal or gas grill, hibachi, or portable gas camp stove indoors.
- When barbequing on your deck or patio, keep the grill away from windows since the smoldering charcoal embers produce large amounts of CO that can enter your house. Even a propane barbecue emits CO.
- Never use a generator indoors.

Be aware of other causes of carbon monoxide buildup.

Never start or run a car, truck, motorcycle, gasoline-operated tractor, lawn mower, snow blower, etc. in a closed garage, especially if the garage is attached to the house. Even if the garage door is partially open, a pocket of CO can form. In addition to potential carbon monoxide poisoning, the fumes caused by running these vehicles and equipment are dangerous, as a random spark can cause an explosion and fire.

To reduce the severity of an explosion or fire in the event of a gas leak, don't store flammable liquids (gasoline, paints, solvents, etc.) in your house or garage. Keep combustible items (rags, paper, etc.) to a minimum and away from appliances.

How to Prevent Carbon Monoxide Poisoning

If the pilot light goes out on your appliance, close the appliance's shut-off valve. Have it checked out by your service company. Don't attempt to turn it on without professional help.

If you smell the rotten egg odor or hear the hissing sound of a gas leak, alert family members and get out of the house. Call 911 from outside the house.

Make sure your child knows not to use the house phone or cell phone or turn lights or appliances on or off in the event of a gas leak. Electric currents in phones and switches can ignite the fumes, sparking an explosion. Explain about this danger.

When the gas company shuts off the gas to your house, don't turn it back on. Only a professional should perform this step.

Remember: keep your house CO alarmed to help keep your family unharmed.

CHAPTER 12

How to Call for Help in an Emergency

IN THE READING ROOM

Polly lives with her grandmother in a house right in town. Her grandmother is elderly and doesn't drive. Polly is in third grade and walks to school alone because the school is right down the block. Grandma stands outside the house and watches Polly get to the front door of the school. Polly crosses the street with the help of a crossing guard.

Grandma shops for groceries and other necessities by walking to the stores in the neighborhood. Grandma likes to take Polly out for lunch on Saturday and to a movie on Sunday afternoon.

Sometimes Grandma feels tired and rests on the sofa in the living room. Polly watches over her and brings her water or iced tea or snacks. Grandma worries that in an emergency, she might need help.

She teaches Polly what to do if such an emergency occurs.

Grandma tells Polly, "In an emergency, call 911 for help. If I'm unable to call, *you can make the call.*"

Polly asks, "How will I know when to call 911?"

Grandma tells her, "In a true emergency."

"But Grandma, how will I know if it's a true emergency?"

Grandma tells her the following: "Fire, flood, serious accidents, or illnesses are true emergencies. If a family member or other person at home is unconscious or unable to get up after falling, call 911 at once. A scraped knee, lost pet, or a stolen scooter are significant matters, but are *not* true emergencies."

How to Call for Help in an Emergency

"When you call 911, an operator will answer and refer your call to the appropriate place, which may be the police department, fire department, a hospital, doctor, or Emergency Medical Service. They will send firefighters or police officers and/or medical workers to your home to help."

"If you see an accident or come upon someone who is badly hurt or very sick, ask an adult to call 911. If no adult is around, you can make the call."

Polly asks, "When I call 911, what do I tell the operator?"

Grandma replies, "First of all, be calm and speak clearly. You're a big girl and can do this. Tell the operator your first and last name, your address (house number, street name, and town). If the emergency is not at home, tell the operator the location to the best of your ability. The operator will ask, 'What kind of emergency is it?'"

"Give the reason for your call. Say, 'Fire' or, 'My grandma fell and can't get up,' or 'Grandma is on the floor and she's not awake.' Tell the operator if more than one person is sick or hurt. And Polly, don't hang up until you are told to do so."

Grandma wants all children to know how to be prepared for an emergency. She thinks the following tips will be helpful:

- A first-aid kit should be kept handy, and you should be taught basic first-aid procedures.
- You and your family should take a professional course in first aid, CPR, and use of an AED (automated external defibrillator). This will give you the potential to save a person's life.
- Keep a list of important phone numbers next to each phone. The numbers should include:
    - fire department
    - police department
    - hospital emergency room
    - poison control center
    - local drug store (an all-night one if there's one nearby).
    - your doctor
    - your parents' doctors
    - neighbors and relatives
    - your parents' cell phone, work phone, and pager numbers.
- Learn how to make these calls. If you have a cell phone, have someone program these numbers into it.

Remember: when all is said and done, the most important number to know is 911.

CHAPTER 13

What to Do If Someone Is Choking

IMPORTANT INFORMATION FOR THE PARENT, GRANDPARENT, OR OTHER CAREGIVER

As I'm writing this handbook, a young woman choked to death on a hotdog at a ballgame. I don't know how it happened, but I do know choking incidents happen frequently. A prominent businessman in our community died after choking on a piece of chicken. The other day, a woman said she saved her own life by doing abdominal thrusts on herself.

Every single day I caution my five-year-old granddaughter about *safe eating habits*. Then I took it one step further. I signed up our family for an American Heart Association CPR AED course. When I called to register, I told the person on the phone that my granddaughter was five years old and wanted to take the course with us. He said they had never taught anyone that young, but there were no age restrictions. We took the three-hour course and, in one evening, my granddaughter learned how to do compressions and rescue breaths on adults and infants, plus how to use the AED (automatic external defibrillator). In a practice emergency situation, I called out, "Get the AED," and she brought it over, unpacked it, turned it on, placed the pads on the victim's chest, followed the oral instructions to give a charge, and returned to giving compressions. She did everything that was required of an adult and received a card stating so. Every child should have the opportunity to acquire these skills.

What can you do to protect your child from choking?

Parents must teach young children careful eating habits. They must prepare the foods they serve children in a way that reduces the prospect of choking.

The most common foods to be concerned about are hotdogs, steak, chicken, raw carrots, nuts, and grapes. Don't consider this list as all-inclusive. I'm sure that if you think about it, you can come up with other foods that can be equally dangerous. These foods should be cut into very small pieces before serving your child.

Hard or chewy candies, gum, and popcorn are other choking hazards. Nonfood items, such as toy parts, magnets, beads, coins, etc. can be even more dangerous.

There are steps you can take to reduce the likelihood of choking.

IN THE READING ROOM

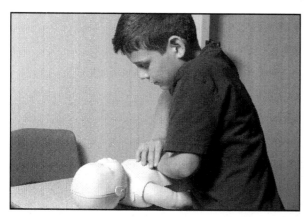

Polly came to live with her grandmother when she was less than two years old. She had just learned how to eat solid foods, and Grandma wanted to avoid any choking episodes, so she cut Polly's food into tiny pieces and watched her as she ate each meal. As Polly grew older, Grandma made up rules for Polly to follow to keep her safe.

She asks, "Polly, did you ever feel like you were choking? Isn't it a scary feeling? There are things you can do to prevent choking. Please, please learn and follow these rules."

- Stay seated while eating. Eat small bites of food at a time. Don't talk, laugh, jump, or run around with food in your mouth.
- Don't run or jump around while sucking on hard candies, chewing gum, or eating chewy candies or popcorn.

- Don't put small toys or toy parts in your mouth. Swallowing nonfood items is a major cause of choking.
- Never put batteries or magnets in your mouth. If swallowed, they can cause choking as well as serious internal damage.

Grandma tells Polly that choking occurs when a piece of food or other object gets stuck in your throat or windpipe. It obstructs the airway, so air can't flow in and out of the lungs.

Polly asks, "What should I do if I start to choke?"

Grandma responds, *"Get immediate attention.* Let someone know, whether it's your parent, grandparent, caregiver, sibling, teacher, playmate, or other nearby person, by gesturing—grabbing your throat—that you are choking."

"Bang on the table. Stamp your feet. Kick something. Do anything to get noticed. Then point to your throat. *The universal sign for choking is to cross both hands over your throat with your mouth open wide."*

What to Do If Someone Is Choking

IMPORTANT INFORMATION FOR THE PARENT, GRANDPARENT, OR OTHER CAREGIVER

How can you tell if your child is choking?

Sometimes, the blockage is *partial* and the child can speak and cough. Ask the child to cough to try to dislodge the object.

If the child clutches his or her throat and can't talk or cough, the likely cause is choking. Other signs of choking are: noisy breathing; skin, lips, and nails turning blue; unconsciousness. If these symptoms are occurring, *yell for help. Start administering CPR (cardiopulmonary resuscitation). Get someone nearby to call 911 and, if no one else is around, start CPR and then call 911 as you administer CPR.*

What should I do until help arrives?

Don't reach into your child's throat to feel for the object. You could make it worse by lodging it more firmly into the airway.

There are two recommended methods of dislodging a stuck object. The American Red Cross recommends a "five-and-five" method to free the stuck object: five back blows followed by five abdominal thrusts. They tell you to repeat this procedure until the object is displaced. The American Heart Association recommends using the abdominal thrust method only.

Learning how to use both these techniques should offer greater protection.

<u>Back blows.</u>
Stand or kneel behind the child and bend the child slightly forward, holding one arm across the chest. Take the bottom part (heel) of your other hand and strike the child sharply on the back between the shoulder blades. Do five separate back blows. Check the child between each one.

Abdominal thrusts (also known as the Heimlich Maneuver).
While standing or kneeling behind the child, wrap your arms around the child's waist. Bend the child slightly forward. Make a fist and press the thumb knuckle of your fist just above the child's belly button and well below his breastbone.

Grab your fist with your other hand and give five, quick, hard inward and upward thrusts into the belly, as if you're trying to pick up the child. Do five separate thrusts and check the child between each. If the child becomes unconscious, stop!

If you're using the Red Cross *alternating* "five and five" procedure, repeat the alternating back blows and abdominal thrusts, until whatever is causing the choking is forced out of the child's throat or the child starts coughing. Again, if the child becomes unconscious, stop!

What to Do If Someone Is Choking

If the object is coughed up, check to make sure that it's the whole object. If you're not sure, look in the child's mouth and, if you can, remove anything remaining.

After you administer the thrusts, if the object remains in the child's throat and he or she is unconscious or not breathing, start CPR (cardiopulmonary resuscitation). *Have someone call 911 immediately. If you're alone, start CPR and call 911 as soon as possible.*

Put your face near the child's mouth to check for breathing. If the child is breathing, you'll feel the breath on your cheek. If the child is *not* breathing, follow the below procedure for chest compressions and rescue breaths. Then look into the child's mouth. If you see the object, remove it. If you don't see it or can't take it out, continue CPR until help arrives. If you're in a public place, ask for an AED (automated external defibrillator). If you're at home, the emergency responder should have an AED in the ambulance.

Chest compressions

The following are highlights from the *2011 American Heart Association Student Workbook on Health and Safety* regarding recommended procedures for performing CPR on children. A child is defined as someone older than one year but one who has not reached puberty.

These techniques should not be used on an infant. There is a modified version to be used on children under one year of age.

When do you give CPR?

CPR is given to someone whose heart has stopped pumping blood. *Pushing hard and fast on the chest to pump blood to the brain and heart is the most important part of CPR.*

If you are called upon to perform CPR on a child that is not responding, start CPR at once. If another person is with you, have him call 911.

Place the child on his back on a rigid, flat surface. Move upper body clothes out of the way. Put the heel of one hand on the lower half of the breastbone. Push straight down about two inches at a rate of at least one hundred compressions per minute. After each compression, let the chest come back to its normal position. If you can't push down about two inches with one hand, use two. Put your other hand on top of the first for added pressure. Compressions are important and doing them correctly is tiring. If there is another person who knows CPR available, take turns, switching every two minutes.

Usually, a child's heart stops because she can't breathe or is having trouble breathing. For this reason, it's important to give breaths as well as compressions to the child. Your breaths need to make the child's chest rise. When you see the child's chest rise, you know the child has gotten enough air. While compressions are the most important part of CPR, giving breaths will help even more.

Before giving breaths, you need to open the airway. Put one hand on the child's forehead and the fingers of your other hand on the bony part of the child's chin. Open the airway by tilting the head and lifting the chin. While holding the airway open, pinch the child's nose shut. Take a breath and cover the child's mouth with yours. Give two breaths (blow for one second each). Watch for the chest to rise as you give each breath.

If the chest doesn't rise, reopen the airway by allowing the head to go back to the normal position. Then open the airway again by tilting the head and lifting the chin. Give another breath, checking to make sure the chest rises. Don't interrupt compressions for more than ten seconds to give breaths. If the chest doesn't rise within ten seconds, begin pushing hard and fast on the chest again. Repeat sets of thirty compressions and two breaths. If you are alone, you are advised to call 911 after performing five sets of thirty compressions and two breaths and to continue sets of 30:2 until help arrives.

How to do the abdominal thrusts on yourself.

Find something waist high that you can bend over—a desk, table, chair, railing, counter, or dresser. Place your fist with your thumb knuckle facing your body, just above your belly button. Grasp your fist with your other hand, lean over the hard surface and give quick, hard, inward and upward thrusts into the belly until the object is dislodged.

Teach your child how to do abdominal thrusts on himself or herself. Take a professional first-aid/CPR/AED course with your whole family.

Part III

Personal Dangers

CHAPTER 14

How to be Safe on the Internet

IMPORTANT INFORMATION FOR THE PARENT, GRANDPARENT, OR OTHER CAREGIVER

The Internet is an integral part of every child's life, easily accessed in so many ways. The web is loaded with terrific children's games, puzzles, quizzes, videos, and more. It combines learning and fun, but a child needs to be properly supervised when using it. Internet safety lessons are a must as soon as your child learns to activate a computer, laptop, tablet, or cell phone.

Never let your child freely roam the Internet. Oversee online activities and designate "favorite" websites that your child knows are OK to view. Always scrutinize a new site to make certain the content is age-appropriate.

At the preschool and early elementary school level, instruct your child in the basics of Internet safety. Tell your child never to enter personal information, such as name, age, phone number, or address, on a site. If the site requires the child to "register" or "sign up," move on to another site that permits play without restrictions. There are many of these available. If a website requires a password, make sure the child knows never to tell the password to anyone other than the parents.

At this early stage, it isn't likely that your child will enter chat rooms or other adult sites. However, it's never too soon to tell your child, "Don't send your picture or provide personal information to strangers." Once the picture or information is out there, it will remain there forever.

Make it clear that your child should never open an e-mail from a stranger.

Learn how to set up parental controls on your computer and smartphones.

CHAPTER 15

How to Prevent Bullying

IMPORTANT INFORMATION FOR THE PARENT, GRANDPARENT, OR OTHER CAREGIVER

There are dozens of words synonymous with bullying: harassing, tormenting, baiting, taunting, provoking, mocking, ridiculing, humiliating, and disparaging are just a few. They're all means of *verbal* abuse, carried out by one or more persons in front of other members of their peer group. Bullying can manifest itself in the form of *physical* abuse as well.

Most bullies suffer from low self-esteem. They are seeking attention, striving for popularity, or, perhaps, emulating their family's dysfunctional behavior. A bully can be any age. For our purposes, we are dealing with school-age bullies.

Bullies need to feel powerful and admired. Frequently, they fulfill these needs by exploiting others. There is usually no particular relationship between bully and victim. The bully can be a family member; part of the victim's peer group, sports team, or club or even a total stranger.

What I'm talking about isn't playful teasing. Bullies *intend* to inflict emotional harm on their victims. They don't care about the victims' feelings. Bullying can take place anywhere and anytime, but usually occurs in front of an audience. Most bullying starts at school but can spread to more wide-ranging locales and, ultimately, to the Internet (cyberbullying) for the widest audience of all. Perhaps one of the worst things about cyberbullying is that it invades the home, the one place where a child should feel secure.

To the victim of a bully, school can feel like a prison where freedom is curtailed. A child who goes to the authorities can expect reprisal from the bully, and going "AWOL" results in the fear of administrative sanctions.

Most contemporary conversation on the topic focuses on curbing the bully's behavior through bystander (witness) intervention and teacher, staff, student, and public awareness. In this handbook, the focus is on making your child *bullyproof*.

Who becomes a victim?

How to Prevent Bullying

The bully handpicks a target, not because of any animus between them, but simply because the particular child exhibits characteristics that fit a "victim" profile. Potential victims are *not* physically threatening. Those who are physically imposing and could easily subdue the bully don't have the requisite mental or emotional state of mind to do so.

If we attempted to profile potential victims, we might use clichés: loners, children who were easily hurt, who never learned to stand up to others; who don't understand the concept of *words will never harm me*, and who never developed the self-assurance necessary to let things roll off their backs. Indeed, if the bullying goes on for an extended period and others in their peer group embolden the bully, victims may begin to believe they deserve the torment inflicted on them.

Once the bully selects a candidate with the requisite traits, any number of pretexts will be used to torment the potential victim. Victims may be:

- new kids in school
- smaller, younger, fearful, self-conscious, chubby, skinny, or clumsy
- of a different religion, ethnicity, or nationality
- smarter, in some cases, or better students, or have special talents that distinguish them from their peers
- experiencing gender or sexuality concerns.
- disabled
- from a single-parent family.

If you think you can stop the bullying by attempting to overcome these outward differences, you're headed in the wrong direction. You have to overcome the victim's inner shortcomings to make him less vulnerable and, therefore, a less desirable target.

Bullies have a lot of tools at their disposal:

- They can say cruel and demeaning things to victims in front of others.
- They can ostracize them by refusing to let them eat lunch with them.

- They can keep them out of a pick-up ball game or other activities.

Once bullies succeed in intimidating their victims, they may escalate their assault by threatening, coercing, daring, hazing, or extorting. They may resort to physical abuse: hitting, kicking, hair pulling, shoving, or inflicting other bodily harm.

Ultimately, they may exploit the bully/victim relationship on the Internet, disparaging their victims via instant messaging, e-mailing, texting, and making malicious use of social network sites.

How to *bullyproof* your young child.

Bullies are in their glory when their victims exhibit fear and humiliation. To *bullyproof* children, it's essential that their personas do *not* match the "victim" profile. Bullies are looking for victims who will put up *zero* resistance. Virtually any vigorous response should deter them, and send them looking elsewhere. The would-be victims, however, should not use retaliatory language or physically strike out at the bullies. This type of response will put the potential victims and bullies into the same camp, resulting in a loss of sympathy or empathy for the victims from potential interveners.

Children should understand, however, that there may be times when they have the right to hurt someone to prevent themselves from being hurt. Fighting should be the last resort, but, if necessary, even if it means breaking the rules, children must defend themselves.

What you can do as a parent?

A close parent/child relationship is essential during these formative years. Develop and nurture a trusting relationship between you and your child. Encourage your child to freely communicate any misgivings, concerns or doubts he may have about himself or his schoolmates.

Praise your child's *efforts*, not just achievements. Encourage your child to take on more challenging activities as he or she matures.

Inspire your child to participate in a variety of social activities, yielding a diverse group of friends who will bolster your child's sense of worth.

Give your child the opportunity to take classes in self-defense (boxing, karate or other martial arts) as early as three years of age. In addition to being trained in the art of self-defense, your child will learn focus, discipline, and self-esteem, and will learn to use the newly acquired skills for protection in dangerous situations, but, *never* to harm someone who has *not* been physically threatening.

How to Prevent Bullying

I can't emphasize enough the importance of self-defense instruction.

Take what your child learns in karate, for example, and reinforce it by regularly practicing "fighting" at home. Becoming comfortable using these "fighting" skills will make your child more confident if confronted. *Those who know how to fight rarely have to do so.*

Children should be given opportunities to participate in gymnastics classes and sports in order to develop physical coordination and respect for their bodies, as well as self-confidence and social skills.

Children should be taught that you only get one chance to stop bullying, and that's at the *onset* of the bully's attack. The longer the bullying continues, the more difficult it will be to end it. As the bully's campaign continues, the more brazen it becomes. The bully acquires collaborators. Children should learn that the right body language and verbal response (not vengeful name calling) can deter a bully. *Look confident and feel confident.*

Teach your child to think about body language. Your child should think about making eye contact, holding his or her head high and standing straight with shoulders back. When confronted, for example, the child could look directly at the bully, reach out to shake hands, and make some positive comment like, "I'd like to try being friends." Or just shrug off any insult by saying firmly, "I'm outta here!" or "Back off" and walking away proudly. A confident response will demonstrate a lack of fear. The child should not bully back, because that will worsen the circumstances.

Your child should stay calm. A lack of confidence should not be reflected in your child's demeanor. Tell your child to put on a good act. Role playing and practicing with a parent in front of a mirror can be helpful.

Children should feel good about themselves and recognize that the *bullies are the ones with the problems, not the victims.*

Your child should make it a practice to lunch with friends, move from class to class with a friend or friends, and, if needed, seek adult help.

A great deal of guidance is offered about how to avoid a bully. It sounds like a good idea in theory, but is not so easy in practice. Unless your child exhibits confidence and coolness through body language and tone of voice when confronted, avoidance efforts may be futile.

The following are some suggested methods of avoidance:

- Find an alternate route to and from school.
- Sit at the front of the school bus, near the driver.

- Go to school with a friend. Eat lunch in the cafeteria with a friend.
- Stay away from isolated areas of your playground during recess. Stay with other kids.

How can parents know if their children are being bullied?

These are some of the signs a parent can watch for. The child may:

- exhibit a change in behavior
- seem sad or frightened
- invent illnesses, from headaches to stomach pains, to stay home from school
- not make eye contact
- stop talking about school and not want to participate in routine activities.
- come home from school looking untidy or with torn clothing or missing possessions, have unexplained injuries, or always be asking for money
- have trouble going to sleep.

What should parents do if their child is being bullied at school? This is the toughest part. Sometimes it seems like a no-win situation.

Before taking any steps, talk to the child about the bullying. What is the bully saying that is hurtful? Does the bully threaten, coerce, and/or exert physical force to extract money or scare your child? Find out when and where it's happening, if other kids are involved, and if they are backing up the bully.

- Keep a record of the time and place of each incident and the names of participants.
- If the situation warrants intervention, tell the child what you intend to do *before* you do it.
- If you plan to contact the school, start with the child's teacher and, if that doesn't work, make an appointment with a school counselor or social worker. If you feel that the school staff is not taking the problem seriously and there is no improvement in the situation, your next option would be the principal and possibly the school board.
- Refrain from interacting with the bully's family. Wait for guidance from the school administration. If you do plan to meet with the bully's family, have a neutral party present, unless you know them personally,
- In extreme cases, local law enforcement may have to be notified. Become familiar with the laws regarding bullying and harassment in your community.

I remember being bullied in the schoolyard in sixth grade because of my religion and the fact that I was a new student to

How to Prevent Bullying

the school. To this day, I remember the names of the bullies. I'd hate to tell you how many years ago this was.

Bullying can have an enduring impact on children. It can affect their academic studies and their physical, social, and emotional well-being for years to come. In some instances, victims never recover.

Bullyproofing your child at a young age can save both you and your child a lifetime of heartache.

The role of the bystander.

The Alliance for Safe Kids based in Yorktown Heights, New York in its web site stopbullying.gov offers recommendations regarding the role bystanders can play to ease the discomfort of the bullying victims. These recommendations include:

- Spend time with them at lunch, recess and other activities.
- Call the person being bullied to provide support and encouragement.
- Help them talk to a trusted adult.

The Alliance is not suggesting that bystanders put themselves in harm's way. Parents should remind their children to intervene only if they can do it safely. They are suggesting that the bystanders set a good example and *not* encourage the bully's behavior by providing him or her with an audience.

CHAPTER 16

Empowering Your Child

IMPORTANT INFORMATION FOR THE PARENT, GRANDPARENT, OR OTHER CAREGIVER

While the primary purpose of this handbook is teach your child how to be safe from external perils, I'd be remiss if I didn't address perhaps the most significant threat to your child's well-being—lack of self-esteem and self-confidence.

Child empowerment should be the number one priority in every family.

How do you instill a sense of confidence in your child?

- Spend quality time together.
- Engender trust.
- Encourage constructive relationships with adults outside the immediate family.
- Make your child feel like an integral part of the family. Encourage participation in meaningful family conversations. Give your child opportunities to express opinions. Discuss, don't argue. Don't criticize. Don't belittle or disparage. Suggest alternative ideas if you think your child is on the wrong track. My five-year-old granddaughter told me that people who love you don't laugh at you. Out of the mouths of babes.
- Motivate your child to take on challenges and reward with praise, not for succeeding, but for trying.
- Instill a love of learning. Make learning exciting and stimulating. Lavishly praise each effort and each triumph.
- Encourage your child to foster hobbies and interests outside of school.
- Let your child feel highly valued by your family. Your children will learn to see themselves through your eyes.
- Show love with time and attention as well as hugs, kisses, and loving words.
- Teach your child the importance of sharing and serving others.
- Develop problem-solving skills by role playing.
- Never compare one sibling to another.

My friend, a mature woman, recounts how her mother compared her to her sister each time they were introduced to an acquaintance. The mother would point to my friend's sibling and say, "This is my beautiful daughter" and then point to my friend and say, "And this is the smart one." A lifetime later and this is what my friend remembers about her mother.

Teach your child the danger of accepting "dares." Tell them never to say yes to dares. Not from classmates. Not from siblings. Not from anyone. Make it clear that the person making the dare does *not* have your child's best interest at heart and is, in fact, hoping the child will fail. Very often dares are dangerous, even life threatening. Your child should recognize, "This person is not my friend" and walk away from a dare. The sooner this lesson is learned, the safer the child will be growing up.

Give your child the skills to feel empowered. Start today!

My granddaughter started taking karate lessons at the age of three and a half. She just turned five, has her third belt, and loves the feeling of achievement. She attends classes three days a week and begs to practice with her daddy at home after class. Yet she never hits anyone, and when asked why she let someone push her without retaliating, she replied, "I didn't want to hurt her."

Let your children know that you're their confidant and protector. Let them know they can tell you anything without consequences. An open dialogue in early childhood will pay off as they mature.

Good luck and safe child.

APPENDIX

SAFE CHILD ~ DANGEROUS WORLD

Review Questions

To Get the Dialogue Flowing with Your Child

CHAPTER 1:
HOW TO STAY SAFE IN A PUBLIC PLACE

TRUE OR FALSE:

1. I can tell a nice stranger from a bad one by looking at the person.

   TRUE _____
   FALSE _____

2. If a stranger says, "Your mommy sent me," I should go with him.

   TRUE _____
   FALSE _____

3. If a stranger tries to touch me, I should scream and run.

   TRUE _____
   FALSE _____

4. It's OK to play hiding games in a store or mall.

   TRUE _____
   FALSE _____

5. If I think a car is following me in a parking lot, I should turn and walk in the opposite direction.

   TRUE _____
   FALSE _____

CHAPTER 2:
HOW TO STAY SAFE CROSSING THE STREET

COMPLETE THE SENTENCE:

1. It is dangerous to talk on a _____ while crossing the street.

2. I can cross in the middle of the block if there is a _____

3. When a signal light is _____, I can cross.

4. When a signal light is _____, I have to wait until it turns green.

5. A yellow signal light means _____.

6. When crossing near a school, a _____ may help me cross the street.

7. I have to look _____, even if I'm crossing on a one-way street.

8. A stop sign is red and has _____ sides.

9. I should never cross between _____ cars.

10. _____ all drivers are safe drivers.

CHAPTER 3: HOW TO STAY SAFE ON OR NEAR A SCHOOL BUS

ANSWER THE FOLLOWING QUESTIONS:

1. Where should I walk if our street doesn't have a sidewalk?

2. Where should I stand when I'm waiting for the school bus?

3. Is it OK to play in the aisle of the bus while it is moving?

4. Why should I look outside, toward the back of the bus, when I get off the bus?

5. Where are the emergency exits on a school bus?

6. Why is it dangerous to wear drawstring sweatshirts when getting on or off the bus?

CHAPTER 4:
HOW TO STAY SAFE IN AN AUTOMOBILE

TRUE OR FALSE:

1. If I am only going a short distance, it's OK not to buckle up.

    TRUE _____
    FALSE _____

2. It's dangerous to ride with a drunk driver.

    TRUE _____
    FALSE _____

3. Booster seats raise me up so I can safely strap in.

    TRUE _____

    FALSE _____

4. It's important for me to learn how to unbuckle my car seat belt.

    TRUE _____
    FALSE _____

5. 5. A car engine gives off oxygen when it is running.

    TRUE _____
    FALSE _____

6. 6. I should never stay in a car alone when the engine is running.

    TRUE _____
    FALSE _____

CHAPTER 5:
HOW TO STAY SAFE AT THE PLAYGROUND

MULTIPLE CHOICE: SELECT THE CORRECT ANSWER:

1. What *not* to wear in the playground:
A. Sneakers
B. Nonslip shoes
C. Flip flops _____

2. I see kids playing rough. I should:
A. Play with them
B. Stay and watch
C. Walk away and tell my parent _____

3. I see kids climbing up the slide. I should:
A. Wait until they stop and then use the slide
B. Climb the ladder and block them
C. Climb up the slide with them _____

4. What is the correct way to swing?
A. Lean all the way back.
B. Stand on the swing.
C. Sit facing front and hold on _____

CHAPTER 6:
HOW TO STAY SAFE OUTDOORS IN THE SUMMER

ANSWER THE QUESTIONS BELOW:

1. Can you name two harmful insects?

   _____

2. If you have an allergic reaction to a sting or bite, what should you do?

   _____

3. What will help keep mosquitoes away?

   _____

4. What should you do if you get bitten by a tick?

   _____

5. Name some outdoor creatures you shouldn't touch.

   _____

6. If a neighbor's dog bothers you, what should your parents do?

   _____

7. Who should your parents call if a stray dog bothers you?

   _____

CHAPTER 7:
HOW TO STAY SAFE IN THE WATER

TRUE OR FALSE:

1. When a storm is coming, but it's not near you yet, the weather service issues a storm watch.

   TRUE _____
   FALSE _____

2. I can go into the ocean even if there is no lifeguard or parent with me.

   TRUE _____
   FALSE _____

3. I should never stand with my back to big waves.

   TRUE _____
   FALSE _____

4. If a friend dares me to swim far out, I should take the dare.

   TRUE _____
   FALSE _____

CHAPTER 8:
HOW TO AVOID ACCIDENTS AT HOME

COMPLETE THE SENTENCE:

1. It's not OK to touch a pot on the _____

2. Don't use a microwave without an _____ present.

3. Climbing on a countertop to reach a high shelf is _____.

4. The window in my room should not have any _____ in front of it.

5. It's _____ OK to play with matches or lighters.

6. An _____ should plug and unplug electronic gadgets.

7. I should never try to remove _____ ashes from the fireplace.

8. I should keep ashes far away from my _____.

CHAPTER 9: ADDITIONAL WAYS TO AVOID INJURIES AT HOME

COMPLETE THE SENTENCE:

1. When walking downstairs, hold the _____.

2. Keep your _____ and _____ away from the door jamb.

3. Don't run in socks on a _____ or _____ floor.

4. Don't run or jump around with _____ or _____ in your mouth.

5. Never play with the _____ on a window shade or blind.

6. Wipe up spills on the floor so you won't _____.

7. Don't run near sliding glass _____.

CHAPTER 10:

HOW TO STAY SAFE IN CASE OF FIRE

TRUE OR FALSE:

1. Every home should have smoke detectors and carbon monoxide detectors on every floor.
   TRUE _____
   FALSE _____

2. If there is a fire in your house, get out as fast as you can.
   TRUE _____
   FALSE _____

3. It's OK to go into the house after you call 911 for help.
   TRUE _____
   FALSE _____

4. It's important to have a family meeting place in emergencies.
   TRUE _____
   FALSE _____

5. If there is smoke in the house, get down low and crawl.
   TRUE _____
   FALSE _____

6. It's OK to hide from a firefighter or other rescue person.
   TRUE _____
   FALSE _____

CHAPTER 11: HOW TO PREVENT CARBON MONOXIDE POISONING

COMPLETE THE SENTENCE:

1. If you smell carbon monoxide, get out of the house and call _____.

2. Name three appliances that may operate on gas.
   _____

3. With its added chemical, carbon monoxide smells like _____.

4. If the heat goes off in your house, never use the _____ for heat.

5. If a car engine is running in a closed garage, the fumes it gives off contain _____.

6. If carbon monoxide fumes are in your house, never use your telephone, cell phone, light switch, or turn any appliance off or on, because a spark from any of them can cause an _____.

155

CHAPTER 12:
HOW TO CALL FOR HELP IN AN EMERGENCY

ANSWER THE QUESTIONS BELOW:

1. What is 911? _____

2. When should you call 911?
   _____

3. What should you say when you call?
   _____

4. What list should your parent keep by the phone?
   _____

5. Is scraping your knee an emergency?
   - Yes _____
   - No _____

6. Is losing your bike an emergency?
   - Yes _____
   - No _____

7. Is a fire an emergency?
   - Yes _____
   - No _____

8. Is someone very sick an emergency?
   - Yes _____
   - No _____

9. Is someone badly hurt an emergency?
   - Yes _____
   - No _____

10. You should stay with the sick or hurt person until help comes.
    - Yes _____
    - No _____

CHAPTER 13:
WHAT TO DO IF SOMEONE IS CHOKING

MULTIPLE CHOICE: SELECT THE CORRECT ANSWER:

1. What common foods can cause choking?

A. Hot dogs
B. Grapes
C. Carrots
D. All of the above _____

2. Is it OK to do the following when eating?

A. Jump around
B. Sit still at the table
C. Run around the house
D. All of the above _____

3. What shouldn't I put in my mouth?

A. Marbles
B. Magnets
C. Small toys
D. All of the above _____

4. What should I do if I start choking?

A. Get someone's attention
B. Grab my throat and open my mouth
C. Do abdominal thrusts
D. All of the above _____

CHAPTER 14:
HOW TO BE SAFE ON THE INTERNET

TRUE OR FALSE:

1. It's OK for you to surf the Internet.
   TRUE _____
   FALSE _____

2. You should have a "favorites" list for safe use on the Internet.
   TRUE _____
   FALSE _____

3. You shouldn't give out personal information like name or phone number on any websites.
   TRUE _____
   FALSE _____

4. It's OK for you to put your picture on the Internet.
   TRUE _____
   FALSE _____

5. A password should be a secret between you and your parent.
   TRUE _____
   FALSE _____

6. It's not necessary to have parental controls on my computer.
   TRUE _____
   FALSE _____

CHAPTER 15:
HOW TO PREVENT BULLYING

TRUE OR FALSE:

1. A bully looks for a victim with low self-esteem.
   TRUE _____
   FALSE _____

2. Bullies really don't want to harm their victims.
   TRUE _____
   FALSE _____

3. A bully will be reluctant to pick on a child who shows self-confidence.
   TRUE _____
   FALSE _____

4. Bullies can spot easy targets by their body language.
   TRUE _____
   FALSE _____

5. Giving children lessons in self-defense will give them confidence.
   TRUE _____
   FALSE _____

6. A child who is being bullied might not want to go to school.
   TRUE _____
   FALSE _____

7. If the bullying doesn't stop, the parent should notify her teacher.
   TRUE _____
   FALSE _____

CHAPTER 16: EMPOWERING YOUR CHILD

TRUE OR FALSE:

1. Children should be seen and not heard.
   TRUE _____
   FALSE _____

2. Children should be given the opportunity to express their views.
   TRUE _____
   FALSE _____

3. It's important to have hobbies and interests outside of school.
   TRUE _____
   FALSE _____

4. Reward your child for trying, not just for succeeding.
   TRUE _____
   FALSE _____

5. A child should learn problem-solving skills.
   TRUE _____
   FALSE _____

6. Parents should not compare siblings. Children should stand on their own.
   TRUE _____
   FALSE _____

SAFE CHILD, DANGEROUS WORLD

ANSWER SHEET

CHAPTER 1. HOW TO STAY SAFE IN A PUBLIC PLACE

1. F, 2.F, 3.T, 4.F, 5.T.

CHAPTER 2. HOW TO STAY SAFE CROSSING THE STREET

1. Cell phone
2. Crosswalk
3. Green
4. Red
5. Caution, don't walk
6. Crossing guard
7. Both ways
8. Six sides
9. Parked
10. Not

Safe Child ~ Dangerous World

CHAPTER 3. HOW TO STAY SAFE ON OR NEAR A SCHOOL BUS

1. On the side of the road facing traffic
2. On the sidewalk away from the curb
3. No, you must sit in your seat while the bus is moving.
4. A car may be trying to pass the bus on the shoulder of the road.
5. Rear door, windows, roof hatch
6. The strings can get caught on something.

CHAPTER 4. HOW TO STAY SAFE IN AN AUTOMOBILE

1. F, 2. T, 3. T, 4. T, 5. F, 6. T.

CHAPTER 5. HOW TO STAY SAFE AT THE PLAYGROUND

1.C, 2.C, 3.A, 4.C.

CHAPTER 6. HOW TO STAY SAFE OUTDOORS IN THE SUMMER

1. Bees, wasps
2. Tell an adult, apply first aid, and see a doctor, if necessary.
3. Remove standing water
4. Have your parent or caregiver remove it carefully.
5. Birds, bats, squirrels, moles
6. Complain to the dog owner.
7. Dog catcher or town animal control officer.

ANSWER SHEET

CHAPTER 7. HOW TO STAY SAFE IN THE WATER

1.T, 2.F, 3.T, 4.F

CHAPTER 8. HOW TO AVOID ACCIDENTS AT HOME

1. Stove
2. Adult
3. Dangerous
4. Furniture
5. Not
6. Adult
7. Hot
8. House

CHAPTER 9. ADDITIONAL WAYS TO AVOID INJURIES AT HOME

1. Banister
2. Hands, feet
3. Slippery or wet
4. Food, candy
5. Cord
6. Slip and fall
7. Doors

CHAPTER 10. HOW TO STAY SAFE IN CASE OF FIRE

1. T, 2. T, 3. F, 4. T, 5. T, 6. F

CHAPTER 11. HOW TO PREVENT CARBON MONOXIDE POISONING

1. 911
2. Hot water heater, stove, clothes dryer
3. Rotten eggs
4. Stove
5. Carbon monoxide
6. Explosion

CHAPTER 12. HOW TO CALL FOR HELP IN AN EMERGENCY

1. Emergency number to reach the police, fire department, and emergency medical service
2. When you have an emergency
3. What the emergency is and your name, address, and telephone number
4. All emergency phone numbers, such as doctors, hospitals, family members, and other people you want to reach in an emergency
5. NO
6. NO
7. YES

ANSWER SHEET

8. YES
9. YES
10. YES

CHAPTER 13. WHAT TO DO IF SOMEONE IS CHOKING

1. D, 2. B, 3. D, 4. D.

CHAPTER 14. HOW TO BE SAFE ON THE INTERNET

1. F, 2. T, 3. T, 4. F, 5. T, 6. F

CHAPTER 15. HOW TO PREVENT BULLYING

1. T, 2. F, 3. T, 4. T, 5. T, 6. T, 7. T

CHAPTER 16. EMPOWERING YOUR CHILD

1. F, 2. T, 3. T, 4. T, 5. T, 6. T

Made in the USA
Lexington, KY
07 November 2013